DETECTIVE CAMINADA'S CASEBOOK

MEMOIRS OF MANCHESTER'S SHERLOCK HOLMES

JEROME CAMINADA

Edited by
ANGELA BUCKLEY

MANOR VALE ASSOCIATES

This edition published in 2017 by
Manor Vale Associates

Cases first published in 1895 in *Twenty-Five Years of Detective Life*,
published by John Heywood

Paperback ISBN: 978-0-9935640-4-8
Ebook ISBN: 978-0-9935640-5-5

Manor Vale Associates

6 Merthyr Vale
Reading RG4 8QQ

'The stories related in the following pages - unlike so many of the so-called stories of detectives - are founded on facts, and are, from first to last, and in all their details, truthful histories of the crimes they purport to describe, and of the detection and punishment of the criminals.'

Jerome Caminada, *Twenty-Five Years of Detective Life*, 1895

CONTENTS

PREFACE

I came across Detective Jerome Caminada for the first time while I was researching my roots in our shared city of Manchester. The nineteenth century real-life sleuth was a member of the same ex-pat Italian community in Ancoats as my great-grandparents. Furthermore, in a more dubious link, one of my English ancestors kept a 'house of infamous notoriety' on Caminada's beat in Deansgate, when he first joined the force as a constable. I studied Caminada's memoirs for my biography, *The Real Sherlock Holmes: The Hidden Story of Jerome Caminada*, and was enthralled by his adventures.

Jerome Caminada was born in 1844 in the slums at the heart of the city, opposite the Free Trade Hall. His parents were immigrants; his father was a cabinetmaker from Italy, and his mother's family was Irish. Despite the loss of his father and five of his seven siblings, he survived an impoverished and precarious childhood to join the Manchester City police force, at the age of 23. After patrolling the infamous rookeries, where crime was rife, Caminada showed such aptitude for detective work that he was promoted into the

Detective Department, where he served for almost 30 years, rising to the rank of superintendent.

In 1895, towards the end of his career, Jerome Caminada published the first volume of his memoirs. Although he stated that he wrote up his cases following 'the persuasions of many friends', police detective autobiographies had become popular towards the end of the century, partly to counteract the rather plodding image of the police officer often portrayed in the newly-emerging genre of detective fiction. Caminada's first volume of memoirs comprises some fifty cases from his experience of policing the streets of his city. I have selected 22 of the very best examples, which demonstrate the brilliance of Caminada's detective abilities and which led to his becoming known, during his lifetime, as Manchester's Sherlock Holmes. I have reproduced his words exactly, reducing slightly three of the cases to remove some irrelevant material.

My personal selection includes forgers, pickpockets, confidence tricksters and gambling racketeers. Caminada tells of his encounters with some extraordinary criminals, such as Robert Horridge, a notorious burglar who became the detective's arch rival, and whom he faced in a deadly confrontation. Another was the Reverend Edward Silverton, a well-respected Baptist minister and quack doctor who peddled fake potions to the worried well. Caminada also dealt with public disorder and unrest, battling with the Manchester Anarchists, who immortalised his efforts in a ballad, and the supporters of an MP who was on the run from justice in Ireland.

In addition to criminal cases, Caminada's writings provide an insight into life in Manchester in the aftermath of the Industrial Revolution and the struggles of the poorest inhabitants of the city, many of whom were forced to resort to crime in order to survive. His reminiscences are as much social history as the diary of a police officer. Jerome Caminada relates his experiences with humour, compassion and with all his expertise as one of the finest detectives in the history of Manchester.

Angela Buckley

2017

A BEGINNER IN UNIFORM - MEETING A TARTAR

One night whilst on duty, in uniform, in John Dalton Street, Deansgate, in the year 1868, I was called to by some person, and on turning round to answer my usual "Yes sir," I was asked by some individual, in terms none too polite, "Have I to pay rates and taxes to keep such lazy *fellows* as you walking about the streets?" Without further ceremony or warning he gave me a blow on my nose, which made me reel; but when I turned upon him he took to his heels and ran into a beerhouse in Ridgefield.

I was certainly a little nonplussed. To get a violent blow on the nose at 10.30 p.m., on a cold March night, was not a very pleasant experience for a beginner, especially as the air was keen, and frozen snow was lying on the ground.

I walked away from the beerhouse door, to return to my patrol in John Dalton Street, and just as I reached the corner of Ridgefield, and was turning into John Dalton Street, without the slightest warning I received a violent blow on the ear, whilst a voice exclaimed, "Take that! How do you like it?" I didn't like it at all, and turning round saw that the person who had delivered the blows was the man who had given me the one on the nose a few minutes before. On my making for him, he pursued the same tactics as before and rushed into the beerhouse with me at his heels. Opposite the front door of the house there was a flight of stairs leading to a club-room of the very Loyal Order of ____. Up these stairs my assailant rushed, but I managed to clutch him round the legs, and to drag him to the bottom. In the scuffle he managed to get my hand into his mouth, and began to bite away in right good fashion. Fortunately, he had no teeth, but he worked away so vigorously with his gums that I could feel the pain for weeks after. A crowd had by this time collected round the door. My man was a good deal heavier than I should like to tackle today; but at last I got fairly hold of him, and dragged him through the crowd to the Police Station.

On the Monday morning, the prisoner, one Quinn, who kept a beerhouse, was placed in the dock of the Police Court. He asserted that I had been to his house and demanded beer, and because he would not give it to me I had threatened to have it in for him.

It was clearly shown, however, that at the time he stated I was in his house, I was on special duty elsewhere, with a number of other officers. He then fixed another time; but this served him no better, as it was before I joined the police; so he was fined 10s. 6d., with 5s. costs.

Though the matter was no joke at the time, I often smile when I come across my friend, the beerhouse-keeper Quinn.

MY BAPTISM OF BASE COINERS

During the year 1869 a large number of complaints were made respecting base coins, which had been put into circulation amongst the shop-keepers of the City of Manchester.

Many persons were taken into custody for tendering these coins, but as the complaints increased, special orders were issued to run down the coiners, and I was one of the officers told off for this particular duty. Among the persons I was directed to "shadow" was "Brocky Dave", a notorious criminal, who had been seen in company with a well-known coiner, and who, it was suspected, was in communication with the base coin mint.

One Saturday evening about six o'clock I noticed "Dave" coming down Mason Street, and on getting nearer to him saw that he was carrying a box, from which a number of wires projected. As I followed him down one side of Shude-hill Market I saw that two other officers were also on his track. I did not, however, attempt to speak to them, and we all three followed him through the city to Hardman Street, Deansgate, where he bolted down a passage and ran up a pair of stairs leading to the upper storeys of one of the houses. I found shelter behind a handcart standing near, and after a while I observed both the officers, neither of whom had seen me, go away. About two hours later another notorious thief, known by the name of "Raggey Burke," left the premises "Dave" had entered, and turned in the direction of Salford. When he arrived opposite the Commercial Hotel, in Hardman Street, I saw him take something from his pocket and examine it under a lamp. Whilst he was thus engaged I walked up and arrested him. As soon as he saw me he flung a parcel to the ground, and a working man standing close by called my attention to it. The interference of the stranger so disgusted "Raggey" that he said he was not a man or he would assist a fellow when he saw him in the lion's mouth, and not "snitch" (tell) upon him; upon which the other retorted by telling him to go and work for his living like other people, then "he would not have hold of you."

Whilst this was going on I picked up the parcel, and on taking "Raggey" to the Police Station and searching him found three base half-crowns in his pocket, and sixteen others in the parcel.

"Where do you live?" I asked.

"You know all about it," he replied.

It soon became evident from his conversation that he suspected "Dave" had "rounded" upon him. I did not undeceive him, and on mentioning that I had seen "Dave" go into the same house, he replied, "Yes, he gave you the strength of it. I can see now why he went for the battery, and his game in going to Marshall Street." This was capital news for me. At this time I had never seen a "battery," though I had often heard of them, so taking two other officers with me I immediately set off for the house mentioned. Arriving there, I took off my shoes, and leaving them with the officers who were standing in the passage, or hovel, I crept upstairs in my stocking feet. In the back room of the first floor I heard someone talking, and on carefully examining the partition found it consisted of wood. I discovered a small opening between the boards, and through it could see "Dave" and "Scotch Jimmy," a third well-known character, busily working at something which lay upon a table before them. Listening, I found that they were talking of the recent death of a well-known receiver of stolen goods.

Returning quickly to my colleagues I put on my boots, and we all three crept quietly upstairs. Flinging myself with my whole weight against the door it burst open, and in we all three flew. A few seconds sufficed to secure the coiners. Leaving an officer in charge until I had taken the prisoners to the Detective Office, I returned, and, searching the premises, found the battery to which "Raggey Burke" had referred, a number of moulds, a quantity of tools, plaster of paris, several bottles of acids, and other things used in the manufacture of base coins.

When the three men were placed together at the Detective Office, "Raggey" was very sore with "Dave," and "Dave" showed a similar feeling towards "Raggey," each believing that the other had informed of him, whilst "Scotty" was wild with both, telling them that they had been using "garden stuff," meaning that they had been giving information.

Being placed in a cell together settled their differences, and on Monday morning when before the Court admitted that it was "a fair cop," especially as one of my colleagues gave evidence of watching "Dave" on his way to Hardman Street the previous Saturday.

The prisoners were sent to the Assizes, and tried before Mr. Justice Brett, on January 15th, 1870, "Raggey" being indicted for having three base half-crowns in his pocket, and the other two for coining, and being in possession of implements for such a purpose. "Dave" and "Raggey" were each sentenced to fourteen years', and "Scotch Jimmy" to seven years' penal servitude.

The previous convictions against "Brocky Dave," whose name was John L___, *alias* Nicholson, *alias* Fletcher, were as follows: - June 28th, 1850, illegally pawning, 42 days; March, 1851, at Liverpool Assizes, robbery, seven years' penal servitude; August 25th, 1856, larceny, six years' penal servitude; February 23rd, 1864, stealing money, six months'; June, 1868, at Manchester Sessions, felony, eighteen months'.

This was the severest blow that the coining fraternity in this quarter had received for many years, and for a long time after there were no complaints. I may add that "Raggey" had served previous terms of four years' penal servitude and ten years' penal servitude, and was one of the convicts tried for the mutiny at Dartmoor about 1865, and for that offence was flogged.

3

A "GHOST" IN A PIANO CASE

One day, a complaint was made at the Manchester Detective Office by a very respectable firm in the City, that music was continually being stolen from the concerts which they held in the Free Trade Hall. The matter was taken into hand, but the pilfering continued. Every concert night music was missing, and no clue could be obtained to the thief.

At length I arranged with the firm to have a large piano box made in such a manner that I could enter it and let myself out whenever necessity required. Holes were bored in such a way that I could see, when inside the case, all that was passing around me. When the box was completed and had been delivered at the Free Trade Hall, I got inside it, no one having the slightest knowledge of its unmusical contents. As the time for the concert drew near, the librarian, who was in charge of the music, took up his position; the musicians commenced to tune their instruments, and everything being in order a move was made for the platform, leaving the worthy knight, who conducted the orchestra, and the librarian alone with the piano box and myself in the ante-room. I had often been told in answer to my inquiries of the trust that was reposed in the old librarian, and not a tittle of suspicion rested on him in the minds of his employers.

The concert commenced at 7.30 p.m., and Sir __ having proceeded to his duties, the old gentleman was then in sole charge of the room.

Everything went on right until the interval of ten minutes at 8.50, when the room was again filled with the performers, bustling, hurrying and tuning their instruments.

The concert was resumed, the ante-room again cleared, and the old librarian and myself were once more together. The concert had proceeded about half-an-hour, when the old gentleman began to be very busy looking over the music.

In a short time I saw by his features that he had come across something which drew his attention and gave him pleasure. After glancing at the piece of music, he looked round, made sure, as he supposed, that he was alone, saw that the doors were closed, and then drew two sheets of music from the pile and put them into his pocket. I remained perfectly quiet. After the concert the room was again filled, the old gentleman was exceedingly pleasant and fussy, with a good word and a nod for everyone, and at length they all dispersed. I was now in a fix. The difficulty with me was how to get out of my hiding place, for a number of the musicians had placed their fiddles and other instruments against the case. To add to my troubles, while I was devising some scheme to release myself, the gasman appeared with the long stick to turn out the gas. I cried out in a suppressed voice, which, coming from the hollow box, made it seem unearthly, "Shift these fiddles." "Oh!" cried the man, starting back, and looking straight at one of the bass fiddles, as if it had addressed him - "What's that?"

I saw through one of the holes in the box that the man was trembling with fright, and perhaps would have run away; but as he received no answer to his question he became re-assured, and again lifted his stick to put out the gas, when I bawled out in right good earnest, "Shift these fiddles from the piano case, man, and let me out. I am no ghost, but flesh and blood like yourself."

The poor fellow, with hair almost standing on end, obeyed, and when I emerged from my temporary prison I saw that he was in a cold perspiration, and almost ready to drop. All the blood having forsaken his face, he looked really more like a ghost than I did.

I had, however, accomplished my task. The pilferer was found out; but the firm declined to prosecute.

I have never since been able to conciliate the Free Trade Hall gasman; nor would Mr. Tennant, the manager, induce him to speak to me.

4

RACECOURSE THIEVES

A CHIEF CONSTABLE ROBBED - HOW I WAS AIDED BY A
SHARPER

During the racing season there is a large class of thieves who attend the principal meetings, not only for the purpose of committing robberies, but for "plucking" any "greenhorn" across whom they may come. The ranks of this fraternity are recruited from the gutter-children, who can be seen in the streets of all our large towns, selling newspapers, matches, and other small articles. Neglected at home, and congregating together, these waifs naturally learn vice from each other. In competition for a living they become shrewd and clever, and once they take to bad ways, rapidly develop into dangerous characters. Another class who supply the ranks of the racecourse thieves is that of the youth of good education, but limited means. Beginning to dabble in sporting matters, he soon over-reaches his resources, and often afterwards getting into trouble and losing his situation, becomes clerk to some book-maker, gradually drifting thereafter into the dangerous business which too often follows.

The racecourse thief is no ordinary criminal. Men of this

stamp are exceedingly cautious. They deliberately prepare their plans; so that when they come to perform their work there is no hesitation from the time they enter upon the business until they dispose of their plunder.

These thieves, as a rule, work in gangs. It is not unusual for one of the "bloke-buzzers," as they are called, when pressing through the entrance turn-stile in the crush at a racecourse, to push off some person's hat. The innocent one puts up his hands to save the hat; the rest of the group gather round, one taking care to put his arms under those of his victim and to hold them in this position, while another quickly abstracts the victim's watch, purse, or pocket-book.

There is no little danger attending the arrest of these thieves on a racecourse, frequented at times by fifty or sixty thousand people interested in betting, many of whom are swindlers, sharpers, and others, who have no sympathy with the police. In such places a great rush can easily be organised; especially when the distance to the police station is a mile or two away. In some cases, however, the prison van is brought on to the course, so that offenders can be locked up at once, and conveyed from the course at the end of the day. At these times it is customary for detective officers to be sent from the principal towns in the kingdom to the race meetings for the purpose of checking the operations of these clever thieves and swindlers.

My first experience of being sent from home was on this very duty. It was the day the Grand National Steeplechase was run at Aintree Racecourse, near Liverpool, in the year 1871. The Superintendent of the County Police placed me with a police constable, who for the occasion had been put in plain clothes. Whilst watching the arrivals at the railway station, I noticed among them two men whose appearance seemed to me to denote that they followed no legitimate calling. Intimating to my colleague that we would follow this couple, I saw them enter one of the booths on the race ground, where they remained until the bell rang for the course to be cleared. Among the welshers and others who came out of the booth, I observed the two we had followed, and told my colleague to keep his eye upon me whilst I "dogged" them. They went towards the grand stand, but stopped opposite the brick bars, upon which is a stand of an inferior class. At this point the space between the bars and the enclosure is considerably narrowed, and being one of the busiest parts of the course a great crowd always congregates there. A man was consulting his race-card, which he held in both hands. One of the men I was watching placed himself at one side of this person and began to consult his own card, at the same time contriving to get one of his elbows underneath that of the victim, thus holding his arm in its place while "covering" his confederate. The latter stood behind, and, putting his arms underneath the elbows of the two men, drew a gold watch from the pocket of the first named. This was all done in much less time than I have taken to describe it.

On the bell being again rung for the horses to come upon the course, the rush of people was so great that I was carried away, and lost both of the light-fingered gentlemen as well as my colleague. It would be impossible for me to attempt to describe my feelings at that moment. Here, on the first occasion when I was sent away from home on special duty, I had just been on the point of making an excellent capture and of earning the approval of my superiors, when all in a moment the opportunity was swept away. Gloomy and despondent I placed myself against one of the stumps, which stood in front of the brick bars, and watched the thousands of people who passed after the race. When the stream had gone by, whom should I see, to my great delight, advancing towards me but the two thieves I wanted. They were looking back, evidently with the intention of discovering whether they were followed. I walked on about fifty yards before them, and coming to a convenient place lay down upon the grass. I watched them go into a field near the railway station, where they disguised themselves in such a manner that they could not, as they thought, be identified. Whilst this change was taking place I caught sight of my colleague, to whom I contrived to get near, and I induced him to take off his overcoat in order the better to hide the palpable outline of a policeman. The thieves bought a couple of oranges from a woman who was standing with a basket near a footpath in the field, and upon the bell being sounded for the next race, instead of making for the courses, they dashed across the field to the railway station. We followed, and on arriving at the station I left my colleague outside, having no fear that my make-up would be discovered. I entered the station after them. They walked up to a person whom I suspected would be the "fence" or receiver of stolen property, and seeing something pass from one to the other I made a rush at the two men, grabbed one in each hand, and dragged them into a wooden shed, which then served as a waiting-room, the "fence" jumping at the same time into a departing train. The suddenness of the attack seemed to paralyse the thieves, and the people on the platform, not knowing what to make of the matter, became alarmed and ran away. This stampede attracted the notice of the officials, and on their running in to see what was the matter, I called upon them in the name of the Queen to assist me. This they did; and on searching the thieves I pulled from the pocket of one a gold watch, minus the bow, about £24 in cash, and a passage ticket to America; while from the other I took about £12 10s. in money.

"To whom does this watch belong?" I asked.

"It is my own," replied the man from whom I had received it.

"Do you generally wear it without a bow?" was my next inquiry. But to this I received no answer.

"What is your business?" I asked.

"A solicitor's clerk," said the first thief, sullenly.

"Where do you come from, and what is your master's name?"

"I decline to tell you" was the curt reply.

The usual threats of pains and penalties followed, and I was to be made to "sit up properly." Disregarding all this bounce I requested one of the railway servants to call in my colleague. To him I handed one of the men, and I myself took charge of the other.

The following day a gentleman who had seen the scuffle at the station informed me that a gentleman who was staying at the same hotel as himself had lost his watch on the racecourse. I waited upon the gentleman referred to, and he identified the watch which I had thus recovered. The prisoners were convicted and sentenced to six months' imprisonment with hard labour.

My first experience of racecourse duty was therefore distinctly encouraging from a detective's point of view.

Some years later I was on duty at the same racecourse, Mr Boyes, now Chief Inspector of the Liverpool Detective Police, being my colleague. We were asked to take charge of the grand stand and its surroundings.

On the first day of the race two robberies were reported. The next day, the "Grand National" was to be run. This event always brings together a large concourse of people. While Mr Boyes and I were inspecting the ring, I saw three men whom I suspected were "working" together. A little further away was an aged gentleman walking with a stick as if troubled with rheumatism. The shortest of the three men, all of whom were made up as "swells," knocked against this gentleman, and before the sufferer could recover from the shock I saw the swell thief put his hand into the gentleman's inside coat pocket.

"Ring," I said to my colleague, meaning that we should disguise ourselves, and this we did immediately, turning to one side for the purpose. I watched the gang over my colleague's shoulder. They took up their position against a gentleman wearing an Albert overcoat. One of the three, a tall, dark, man, wearing a pair of eye-glasses, stood close to him, whilst another of the gang, whose appearance much resembled that of a respectable publican, got behind. This second man pressed forward, while the other, standing upon his toes, as if to see over the people's heads in front of him, held his glasses to his eyes with one hand, and placed the other on the shoulder of the gentleman as if to steady himself. As this was taking place the little "swell," with light-ning speed, unbuttoned the gentleman's coat, felt his pock-ets, but without finding anything.

The gang then separated, but met again a short distance away. After some conversation they went upon the grand stand. As the principal race of the meeting was in progress it caused a great flutter and bustle, everyone being anxious to obtain as good a view as possible, and there was a consider-able crush.

In the crowd was a gentleman, who, as he afterwards told us, had for safety buttoned both his overcoat and undercoat from top to bottom, placing his purse in his inside breast pocket. The same tactics were pursued upon him as in the other case. The little swell boldly unbuttoned both the coats, detached the bar of the gentleman's albert chain from the buttonhole and drew the watch from his pocket with the chain attached and handed it to the tall man, who at once hurried down the stairs. With all their cleverness, however, they had fallen into a trap, for on the receiver's arrival at the bottom I stopped him and gave him into the custody of the Liverpool police. I repeated the operation upon his little companion who followed, and gave instructions that the hands of the men were to be secured until my arrival at the Detective Office. The third man did not come down the stairs until the race was over. He had no sooner made his appearance than I seized him and lifted him completely off his feet, carrying him bodily into the Police Office, a distance of thirty or forty yards away, to the astonishment of a many good people.

As I began to search them, the first arrested inquired, "What do you want?"

"Clocks" (the slang name for watches), I replied. Whereupon the thief took from his trousers pocket a gold repeater watch and albert guard.

"Whose is this?" I asked.

"Mine," said the robber.

"Where did you get it?" was the next inquiry.

"Find the owner," he tauntingly replied.

As the police office was only a temporary shed, and as I was afraid of a rush being made for the purpose of rescuing them, after searching them I handcuffed the three together, and picking up a constable in uniform - a tall, strapping fellow measuring at least six feet three inches in height, and weighing, I should say, from eighteen to twenty stones - I fastened the trio to him by means of a pair of handcuffs.

Whilst these arrangements were being carried out, we were startled by a gentleman rushing into the office, and excitedly exclaiming, "Where is the Chief Constable?" "Where is the Superintendent? I am the Chief Constable of __, and I have just had a gold repeater watch and albert chain taken from my vest pocket, and my purse from my inside coat pocket, on the grand stand."

This confession caused a smile to come over the countenances of the officers present, and the faces of the prisoners showed that they too appreciated the situation. I turned to the Chief Constable, and pointed out to him that his inside coat had been cut under the breast pocket, and his purse extracted in that way. I asked if he could identify his watch, at the same time producing it from my pocket. The appearance of my colleague and myself in our disguise was hardly calculated to command much respect, and the plundered Chief Constable turned sharply upon me with the question, "Where did you get it from?"

This innocent inquiry was too much for the officers present, who immediately burst into a loud fit of laughter, in which the prisoners joined; and this was not diminished when I coolly pointed to the latter with the remark, "You had better ask these gentlemen."

The next day the three prisoners were brought before the Liverpool justices, and pleading guilty, one was sentenced to six months' imprisonment and the other two to three months each.

This story shows that even responsible officers of police sometimes become as easy prey to thieves as other people.

Another time, being on duty at Lincoln Race Meeting, I noticed a man of distinctly "horsey" appearance rush up to a gentleman, who was a captain in the army. He told him, as I afterwards learned, to back a certain horse. The captain wished to have some conversation with his adviser, but the tipster pretended that he had no time, his presence "being required in the stables." He had no sooner left than a man of gentleman-like appearance accosted the captain, and, after some talk in which he informed the officer that he was a bookmaker, asked him what he wished to back? Whilst this conversation was going on, another man came up and put twenty pounds upon a horse, on what is called "the nod" (that is, no money passes at the time but a settlement is made afterwards). Subsequently, a third man appeared on the scene and made a large bet, thus giving the bookmaker the appearance of being a substantial man. The captain was at length induced to back the "tip" which had been given to him, to win ten pounds. The selected horse won, and the bookmaker was ten pounds in the captain's debt.

When the bell for the next race rang, the captain and the bookmaker were surrounded by those confederates of the latter, who were professedly betting largely with him. In due time the "horsey" man from the stables turned up with his "tip" for the captain; and the bookmaker pressed him to back his choice for fifty pounds, as the others had done. The captain, however, declined to put more than ten pounds on the horse.

This time the "tip" was a failure, and under ordinary circumstances the captain and the bookmaker would have been quits. The confederates of the latter appeared upon the scene as soon as the race was over, and in a very short time a large sum of money passed in settlement.

False notes, dummy cheques, and drafts made out to the "man in the moon" were flying about in abundance, whilst the military gentleman was pinned up in the midst of the gang.

After all the others had been settled with the sharper turned to the captain and demanded a settlement from him. The captain protested that he had only backed the horse for £10, and they were therefore quits; but the sharper was not going to let his victim escape so easily. He stuck to it that the captain had backed the horse for £50, and as proof produced his pocket-book in which the bet was entered, the owner's name and that of the club to which he belonged being impressed in gilt letters upon its back.

An appeal to the sharper's confederates standing around soon simplified matters, and judgment was given against the military gentleman, who was pronounced a defaulter on the turf. A general bustle took place, and in this they carried the captain in their midst into a corner. Becoming alarmed, he turned out his pockets, in which he had only £5. But the sharpers were very accommodating - promissory notes or cheques would do - and the captain at last produced his cheque book and made out a cheque for the balance of £35; the £5 he paid in cash, and the £10 he won on the first race from the bookmaker, making up the £50.

During the afternoon the captain mentioned the matter to a friend, and a consultation took place with a detective officer from Nottingham, who undertook to get the cheque book back for the captain. At night a search was made through the billiard rooms, a sharper assisting them.

The latter endeavoured to entice the captain to play at billiards. Of course, the captain had to pay the expenses of his friend, two detective officers, and the sharper assistant. The only result of the search was, that an arrangement was made for the sharper to meet the captain at the entrance to the grand stand, on the Aintree racecourse, during the Liverpool Meeting.

On the following day, the captain was moving about the racecourse, towards the close of the meeting, looking for the sharpers, when up came another horsey-looking fellow, who wanted to give him a "tip" for the Liverpool meeting. One of the detective officers who had accompanied the captain the previous day saw this, and, going up, wanted to know what the fellow wanted with the gentleman. "What's that got to do with you?" asked the tipster. "He has been swindled out of a cheque and five pounds," was the reply. "Who are you?" "I am a detective from Nottingham." "Well, take that, Mr. Detective," said the horsey man, dealing him a violent blow on the nose, which made him reel and covered his face with blood.

Away flew 'horsey," followed by the cry of "stop thief," which being taken up the fellow was soon caught and brought back. The captain was compelled to stay overnight to give evidence, thus adding further to his expense; but of this, however, he thought little compared with the exposure, whilst "horsey" was fined 20s. and costs. I offered to take the case in hand and arrest the men, but the captain begged me not to do so; public proceedings in Court might do him serious injury. He frankly confessed that he deserved all he got for mixing with such fellows, and said it would be a lesson to him in the future. The thieves thus escaped scot free.

My object in mentioning this incident is to expose one of the favourite practices of racecourse swindlers, and to put incautious people a little more on their guard.

IN THE YEAR 1877 I was directed to go on duty at the Goodwood Race Meeting, which, being a great rendezvous of fashion, attracts thieves from all parts of the kingdom. Whilst on the look out for suspicious characters leaving Victoria Station, London, I was accosted by a stylishly-dressed man, carrying a macintosh across his arm. He inquired whether the train about to depart was an express, and whether I knew at what time it was due at Chichester? From the anxiety he showed to get into conversation with me, and also to enter the same compartment - for I had informed him I was going to Goodwood - I was satisfied that he took me for a "greenhorn." Soon after we started he offered me a cigar, and was very communicative as to his affairs. He was, he said, pleased to get away from business. He generally spent his holiday by going to Goodwood and then journeying to the Isle of Wight. He was very glad to think he had got a pleasant companion, though he knew nothing whatever about me. He then began to tell me some pretty little stories as to how men had made large fortunes by betting, and he confided to me the fact that he himself had won £64 at the last Goodwood Races. A small flask of spirits was next produced, and I could have had anything for nothing from him, particularly as I was "not able to give him change for a £5 note, on account of my money being all in bank notes." He always made a practice of drinking out of his flask first, as he confessed, "in order to show friends that it contains no poison!" I wore a travelling cap, my hat, bag, and umbrella being on the rack over my head.

As we neared Chichester I saw that the platform was crowded with people awaiting the arrival of the express, and amongst them I noticed "Besom George," "Flying Gibb," "Keough the Stall," "Brocky Kelly," "Dicky Drag" - the same swell pickpocket who stole the Chief Constable's watch at Liverpool, as before related - and other well-known thieves.

I quickly detected that there was some "move" on, and whilst watching them perform the "ramp" - a sudden rush and bustle in which robberies are committed - a gentleman was almost pushed off the platform. While they were hustling him among them I saw one take his gold watch from his vest pocket. The speed of the train slackening just at the moment I threw open the carriage door, sprang out upon the platform, and seizing two of the thieves dragged them along the platform into the lavatory, which went down a step. The local police seeing the scuffle interfered, and, not knowing me, seized me by the neck; whilst the rest of the thieves, possessing better knowledge as to my identity, bolted in an instant.

In the scuffle the thieves and I went down together. I shouted to the police that I was a detective officer; whereupon they rendered me assistance. Having searched the prisoners, I handed them over to the local constables whilst I examined the train, from which I took three other men who had been concerned in the robbery; but the watch was not found.

Whilst in the lavatory I was followed by my travelling companion, who kindly brought me my hat, bag, and umbrella. I opened the bag without removing it from his hands, and took therefrom a pair of handcuffs.

Seeing these the lower jaw of my friend fell considerably. A look of horror came over his countenance; and though I entreated him to hold the bag for a few minutes, he flung it to the ground with indignation and disgust, and made "strides," as the Yankees say, in double quick march. The five were secured, and when taken before the magistrates all pleaded guilty to stealing the watch. Three of them were sentenced to two months' imprisonment, and the other two to fourteen days each under the Vagrant Act.

I have often been told by some of the London thieves how "Red 'Un," as my travelling companion was called by his shady associates, related to them his experience of entertaining the detective whom he took for a "flat." Even when I jumped from the train "Red 'Un" had no idea of my intention. He thought I was a Britisher indignant at the rough treatment the old gentleman was receiving, and it was only when he saw the "snaps" that he understood the situation.

5

THE REVEREND QUACK

Formerly the mountebank doctor was so constant a visitor at every market-place as was the pedlar with his pack. But almost all our old customs have ceased, and these itinerants are now rarely to be seen at rural gatherings. Many of us remember, some thirty or thirty-five years ago, the awe with which we looked upon one of these celebrated characters, who erected his stage at the fairs and wakes of surrounding towns and villages. The platform was about six feet from the ground, and was ascended by a short step-ladder. On one side was a table, with medicine chest and surgical apparatus displayed. In the centre of the platform was an arm chair in which the patient was seated, and before the doctor commenced his operations he advanced, taking off his gold-laced cocked hat, and, bowing right and left, began addressing the populace which crowded before the stage.

The successor of the "mountebank doctor," though he is more ambitious than his predecessor, resorts to much the same practices, but on an extended scale.

The rude booth at the fair has given way to elaborately

furnished consulting rooms, the amusing speeches to expensive advertisements; and though the pills and the water remain they are bartered for pounds instead of pence.

About the year 1877 I noticed in many papers, especially in certain prints which had a large circulation among religious people, an advertisement recommending a medicine of the Rev. E. J. Silverton's, of Nottingham, called "Food of Foods." This gentleman had, according to his testimonials, performed miracles in the way of removing deafness. He now undertook to cure every disease to which flesh is heir, and offered his advice gratis. As I did not like the look of the advertisement, I determined to get on the track of this reverend benefactor. With this object I addressed a letter to him, stating that I was 32 years of age, a superintendent of a Sunday school, and was very anxious to get married. I described an imaginary disease, asked him to devote his attention to it, and let me have a reply as early as possible. By return of post I received from the reverend gentleman a circular containing further testimonials of his marvellous cures, and the usual questions in such cases convinced me that I was on the track of a quack. I filled up the circular and returned it. Without delay I received a lithographed letter, on which a picture of Solomon's Temple occupied a conspicuous place, and in which the clever gentleman stated that he had preached to 60,000 people during the visit of the Prince of Wales to Nottingham, thus bringing his name into prominence with that of the Prince, in such a manner as to mislead the ignorant into thinking that they were on intimate terms, or that he had preached at the request of the Prince. That my case had received no special consideration was proved by the lithographed letter, which was evidently sent to all applicants seeking the reverend "impostor's" advice. He, however, did not forget to ask for twenty-seven shillings and sixpence as his fees. Convinced that the man was a rogue I carried on the correspondence for a little while longer, and then handed over the whole to a society which was interested in the matter. Further inquiries were made, and these led the reverend gentleman to remove his quarters to London. Nevertheless I kept my eye upon his advertisements, and noticed that he was travelling round the country, visiting the fashionable watering-places during the season, no doubt making a very good thing out of "advice gratis."

In May, 1884, I was extremely pleased to see by the large placards on the hoardings, in various parts of the City and its vicinity, that this "Good Samaritan" was about to bestow the benefit of his large experience upon the poor inhabitants of Manchester, and, like the celebrated "Doctor Boozey," cure the deaf, blind, and lame, if not that incurable disease, according to Boozey, "old age." Like the amusing doctor of our youth, "all pronounced incurables" were invited to apply, notwithstanding "the hospitals and the dirty doctors," and "mid the blessings of Providence, he would make short work of it and set them upon their legs again." No less a building that the Free Trade Hall had, however, taken the place of the doctor's stall, and, what was still more remarkable, advice was to be given gratis.

Feeling rather sceptical about "advice gratis" paying the expenses of the Free Trade Hall, the extensive advertising, and the elaborate preparations, I determined to pay the reverend and charitable gentleman a visit for the purpose of solving the mystery, and with this object pretended to be suddenly seized with the gout. Putting on an old shoe and limping into the Free Trade Hall, I was ushered into the presence of a gentleman who was called the physician, Mr Silverton not being in attendance. This gentleman asked me what was the matter, when I told him something was wrong with my foot. Instead of looking at it, he examined my tongue, felt my pulse, and asked me a few questions, told me I wanted a good clearing out, and ended by saying that the medicine would be thirty-five shillings.

This is "advice gratis," thought I, with a vengeance. "Do you want it all at once?" I asked. 'Yes," was the firm reply. "Won't you take it by instalments?" I pleaded. "No," was his reply, "but I will take it in thirds - eleven shillings for the medicine and thirteen pence halfpenny for a box of pills would be twelve shillings and three halfpence."

"Had you not better examine my foot?" I enquired, feigning some astonishment. "Oh! there's no necessity," was the physician's reply; "it's only an ordinary case of rheumatism, and we have scores of such cases."

I paid my money and received the medicine. On going out I met the reverend and Good Samaritan himself, and as he asked me if I wished to see him I returned to the consulting room with him, and told him what had passed between myself and the physician, when he said, "We will make a cure of you."

A few days afterwards I paid a second visit to the miraculous doctor, when the same performance was gone through. My tongue was examined instead of my foot; more money was extracted from my pocket, and I promised to make another call. In the meantime I had sent two female detectives to seek advice from the reverend quack, each of whom pretended to be plagued with different complaints. After asking a number of questions, which it would be impossible for me to particularise, and after extracting as much as he could for his fees, Dr. Silverton allowed the ladies to depart with their medicines; these on analysis proved to be exactly the same as that which I had received for rheumatism in the foot, whilst the wonderful "Food of Foods" consisted of nothing but lentils, bran, and brown flour and water. This was the "Elixir for all Diseases."

I now applied for and obtained summonses against the reverend gentleman and his assistant for conspiracy in practising as medical advisers, and as soon as publicity was given to the matter their victims, as is usual in such cases, turned up in great numbers with complaints of their extortionate charges. One poor fellow who visited Silverton for deafness admitted that he was very ill, when the far-seeing and learned parson told him that he was in very good health; but he was afraid to acknowledge it, lest he might charge him for his advice on this head as well as for deafness. He also undertook to cure another man who had been deaf from birth. Many of the patients were examined by the police surgeon and two specialists on the ear, who said it was quite impossible that any of them could ever be cured. There were some most distressing and heartless cases. One poor woman sold the bed from under her in order to obtain advice for her son.

The result of the investigation before the magistrates was that the Stipendiary offered to bind me over to prosecute at the Assizes, but as neither the Medico-Ethical Society nor the Public Prosecutor would take the matter up, and as I thought that the publicity which the matter had obtained would have the effect of putting the public upon their guard, and would be quite sufficient to destroy the system - which was all that was wanted - I declined to carry the case any further at my cost.

My expectations have not been fully realised, for we hear of the reverend philanthropist now-a-days advertising from Ludgate Circus, London. I have forced him again and again to withdraw his advertisement from papers in which it was inserted. I feel confident that I broke the back of this scoundrel, and I shall continue to apply the lash at every opportunity.

When I had additional summonses to serve upon the defendants, I met the reverend gentleman and his assistant walking about outside the office of the solicitor who was appearing for them. I offered the reverend gentleman these summonses, but he declined to accept them; so, taking hold of him with my left hand, I thrust the document into the breast of his vest with my right. "Now you've got them," I said. "I will fight this case to the House of Lords," he replied, "for it's worth £50 a week to me." "You can fight it to the house of d___s," I answered, "if you like, but I will spoil your game;" and raising my hat I bade this would-be gentleman "good morning."

THE FOLLOWING IS an extract from a leading article in the *Manchester Guardian*, Saturday, May 31ˢᵗ, 1884 -

A person styling himself the "Rev. E. J. Silverton, Baptist Minister," was charged at the City Police Court, yesterday, in company with C. C. Mitchinson, his "physician in attendance," with conspiracy to defraud. The "rev." gentleman has taken a room in the Free Trade Hall, and thence issues advertisements announcing his ability to cure nearly every disease to which mankind is subject. One of the "sufferers" attracted by the advertisements was Chief Detective Inspector Caminada, who in his time has had to deal with some very remarkable cases. Caminada presented himself as a "patient," and intimated that something was wrong with one of his feet. The defendant Mitchinson, who is said to be a regularly qualified surgeon, by way of ascertaining the state of Caminada's foot examined his tongue, and prescribed some medicine at the ridiculously low charge, inclusive of the bottle, of 35s. A negotiation between the physician and patient ended, however, in a reduction of the amount, a concession which was possibly due to a desire to benefit suffering humanity even at a pecuniary loss to the benefactor. Caminada subsequently saw the "rev." defendant and received the comfortable assurance that he would certainly be cured. It need scarcely be said that the Inspector's malady was purely imaginary. The medicine he received turned out on analysis to be something usually given for indigestion. It appears, also, that the defendants prescribed an article called the "Food of Foods," which was composed of wheat flour and pulse. It will be seen that they deal largely in "simples." Two women who consulted the defendants for ailments, real in one case and imaginary in the other, had gone to them in good faith. One sought the blessing which was bestowed on the wife of Abraham in her old age, and the defendants for a consideration assisted her with a harmless cough mixture. It is worthy of note that Mr. Silverton has to his own great regret felt compelled to give up the cure of souls in Nottingham in order to undertake the healing of the sick in this and other cities. His advertisements breathe a spirit of high-minded philanthropy which should meet its due reward. The advocate for the defendants submitted that no conspiracy had been proved, and Mr. Headlam took time to consider whether or not he should send the case before a jury.

THE PARSON QUACK AND HIS DAUGHTER

DURING THE MONTH OF JANUARY, 1895, the following advertisement appeared in the Manchester newspapers:-

REV. E.J. SILVERTON'S CURE OF DEAFNESS

Miss Silverton in Attendance

ALL SUFFERERS CAN BE SEEN DAILY at the
MOSLEY HOTEL, PICCADILLY, MANCHESTER from
January 15th until February 2nd.

Hours from II till I, 3 till 5, and 6.30 till 8 o'clock. The Rev.
E. J. Silverton, of Imperial Buildings, Ludgate Circus,
London, cures Deafness, Head Noises, and Discharges from
the Ears without the use of instruments, operations or pain.
Wonderful cures! A person cured after 40 years' deafness. A
remarkable case of a lady at Lincoln, substantiated by a clergyman. A gentleman after 17 years' deafness cured, and one
cured at the age of 90.

Miracles are not performed, but the results witnessed
are the effects of Mr. Silverton's method, and are indis-
putable. Lady sufferers are specially invited to pay a visit,
and all afflicted with deafness should take the opportunity.
Consultations free. A charge is made for the remedy only.

A SIMILAR ADVERTISEMENT HEADED "THIRTY YEARS' Success
among the Deaf" appeared in the *Manchester Evening News*
for March 9th, 1895.

Having some remembrance of the reverend gentleman, I
caused two women to visit the hotel under the pretence of
consulting the quack, but he was not to be seen, being
detained on business in the metropolis. Two detectives,
Sergeants Harris and Wilson, next paid a visit to the rooms.
The former, in the disguise of a cattle dealer, which business

exposed him a good deal to the weather, pretending to be deaf and wearing a pair of blue spectacles, was led into the presence of Miss Silverton, upon whom the mantle of her almost miracle-performing father has evidently fallen, he being still detained in London.

This lady quack, a worthy descendant of her "wonderful-curing" papa, had not been tutored in vain. She had learned her task well. The pseudo deaf Harris was put through an examination, and whilst the two detectives gravely kept their countenances, she as gravely informed them that it was a very serious case, and that unless something were immediately done the poor deaf fellow would lose his hearing altogether. Taking her cue from the blue spectacles, she added for his comfort that his sight was being affected by the disease of the ear. Of course she had to shout very hard to make the "afflicted" Harris understand this; but she scarcely shouted hard enough to make him believe it, for he departed with his friend Wilson, evidently to the lady quack's sorrow, without putting down the money to pay for the course of treatment which was to arrest the disease. Wisely as the siren sang, the charm was scarcely strong enough to make the acute Harris believe he was deaf; but the spell was completely broken when she wanted to make him believe he was going blind; for a blind and deaf detective would have been a rarity indeed, and no wonder the two friends fled from the presence of the "truthful" prophetess, whose papa heads his pamphlet with the quotation from Scripture, "Be not faithless, but believing." Another of his quotations is, "He that hath ears to hear let him hear." The latter is perhaps an unfortunate one, for if this were the case with all people the reverend quack's business would be gone. Fortunately Sergeant Harris "hath ears to hear" and "eyes to see," and heard and saw so well that he came away "faithless" and unbelieving. I would suggest to the reverend gentleman that he should adopt the mottoes: "Deceive not;" "Thy sins will find thee out."

I next determined to pay a visit to the rooms of this good and kind Samaritan myself. Arriving at the "Mosley" I was hoisted by the elevator to the second floor, where I found a number of women, some of whom had come long distances, waiting to receive advice, which was offered "free," "a charge" being "made for the remedy only." Three of these I learned had been deaf from birth, and had been under some of the ablest practitioners in the country, without success; and though they had been informed that their case was hopeless, they had been induced by the pamphlets of this quack to seek his aid in the hope of receiving relief.

This pamphlet is one of the usual quack productions, interspersed with quotations from Scripture - benevolent remarks; and would lead the simple to believe that its author does not seek the "filthy lucre" of this world, but does all out of charity. It is specially designed to bring religious people into the net. It informs us that this reverend "doctor" has "preached the Gospel to thousands in his time," and would lead us to believe that he was first inclined to enter this business for the purpose of making deaf people "capable of hearing the Word." Then, of course, there are the usual wood-cuts and hard-sounding names which no-one but professional men understand; and for the success of his system he points to the number of letters received. And truly these are the most wonderful productions. The Rev. E. J. Silverton, Baptist Minister, quack without diploma, and inventor of the "aural remedy," does not lay claim to "perform miracles;" but if some of these cases are not miracles, it is difficult to say what they are. To cure people of 70 or 90 is a small matter. There is a "wonderful case of a deaf and dumb child;" a "remarkable case of a little girl deaf and dumb;" the cure of a "deaf and dumb boy;" another "wonderful case in Ireland," in which "hearing, sight, and speech" were "all restored;" a case of a person "born deaf and cured after twenty-five years' deafness;" and so on.

The grateful air that runs through these letters must be very gratifying to the reverend gentleman; and there is no mistaking the pious and religious mien of many of them; but there are two or three circumstances connected with these letters which are worthy of note. Only in two cases are the names and addresses given; if more were given they would be of very little use, for the simple reason that they are dated years back, some of them as far back as 1870, and to find people after this lapse of time is almost impossible.

Of the two addresses given one is not in this country, and the other is "Joseph W. Alvey, 64, Cricket Road, Sheffield, dated November 29, 1882," who states - "You can use this letter if you choose in any way to suit your purposes." If anyone is inquisitive enough to inquire they will find that the supposed writer is not known at the address given. In answer to an inquiry relating to this man Alvey, the Sheffield police write - "No. 64. Cricket Road is occupied by a man named Daniels, a boot and shoe repairer. Our officer cannot ascertain anything of the above-named" (Alvey).

We see then the value of these testimonials; but the parson quack is no doubt fully aware that few people trouble themselves to make inquiries. It is not surprising that simple-minded people in want of relief are imposed upon by these accounts of such wonderful cures, and I was not at all astonished to see so many visitors who were "not faithless, but believing;" but I impressed upon them the importance of not parting with any money, unless they received relief, which I felt certain they would not, and I had

the satisfaction of knowing that the lady quack only
succeeded in obtaining money in one case during my stay.
The routine in each case was much the same. Each applicant underwent a sort of examination, and was then told
that the remedy would be supplied on payment of a certain
sum of money. But this parson quack is so clever that he
advertises that "a personal consultation is not necessary."
He thus knocks into a "cocked hat" all those professional
gentlemen who have spent hundreds of pounds on their
education before obtaining their diplomas. No! the Rev. E. J.
Silverton is so clever that all he requires is "a statement
setting forth how long the deafness has existed, if the ears
are mattery or dry, if noises in the ears or head, age, state of
health, etc., etc." What the "etc., etc." is I cannot say, as the
Rev. E. J. Silverton, Baptist Minister, does not inform us; but
when the patient has solved the riddle, and forwarded it on,
the parson quack will "ascertain the probable cost of treatment;" and, when he has pocketed the same, he will undertake to cure the sufferer "without operation or pain." No, the
reverend gentleman scorns to use instruments. How nice to
sit in our carpet slippers, write an account of our ailings,
draw a cheque, send to the Rev. E. J. S., and receive a cure
per return! Her Majesty's Government ought to pass a vote
of thanks to the reverend gentleman; for such a method,
when it once becomes known, cannot fail to increase the
revenue of the post-office. Fancy the postman struggling to
Ludgate Circus, the headquarters of this quack family,
under piles of letters, and the busy scene in forwarding the
remedies to all parts.

My turn at length came, and I was ushered into the
sanctum sanctorum of the female quack by a stylishly-dressed
woman. From the appearance of the room it was quite
evident that effect had been studied. The table was covered

with ear trumpets, and the "aural remedy" was much in evidence. A most fashionably-dressed female, who sat near the fire, rose on my entrance and in the most silvery tones asked what I required. Of course something was wrong with one of my ears, and the lady had some difficulty in making me hear her - in fact, the tones of her voice became anything but silvery before she succeeded. At length she was made to understand, and then I had to undergo an examination. The lady practitioner took up a small lamp, and, lighting it, placed a tube which projected from it into my ear. Now, as the Rev. E. J. Silverton is prepared to cure people without a "personal consultation," I wondered how he was going to make an examination of this kind through the post, or whether Edison had found out some wonderful invention by which it would be done by aid of electricity; but my wondering was brought to an end by the examination being brought to a close, and the lady shouting at the top of her voice, so as to make me understand that "the sense of hearing in my right ear was partly destroyed, and that in the other was entirely gone." I thought it was a bad case, but bad as it was I declined to pay 29s. 6d. for a four months' course, or even 11s. for immediate remedies, and came away fully convinced that Miss Silverton was as big a fraud as her father.

Here is a person who professes to make a minute examination of your ear with an instrument used for that purpose, and by means of that examination pretends to find out that your ears are diseased - in the same way that she found out the blindness of Sergeant Harris by means of his blue spectacles - when nothing at all ails them. What, then, shall we say of these people who profess to work these wonderful cures, and who, to curry favour with the benevolent and charitable, advertise that "any clergyman or minister of the

Gospel may obtain help for any of his congregation and the cost will be made, as far as possible, to suit the circumstances of those for whom such help is obtained." The Rev. E. J. Silverton is a clergyman. He knows the influence of ministers of religion with their flocks, and their desire to alleviate suffering. Their good work, he knows, is better than any advertisement. Therefore it is not surprising to find him in the character of a quack attempting to make people believe that he is acting out of pure benevolence. But whether it is out of charity, or for the gain of "filthy lucre," can anyone say that in the two cases given above the lady quack was not imposing upon the implied credulity of the detectives? And if she could not detect the assumed deafness in either of these cases, but rather pretended to give them the cause, what guarantee is there that she knows anything at all about other cases for which she prescribes? Immediately after consulting Miss Silverton, Sergeant Harris and myself were examined by Dr. Wm. Hislop, the police-surgeon, who could find nothing ailing our hearing, and nothing the matter with Harris's eyes or his throat, which this lady had stated would both be affected by the disease of his ears.

6

AMERICAN BANK THIEVES IN ENGLAND

"BILL THE BRUTE," AND "LONG BILL"

During the summer of 1887, the jubilee year of Her Majesty, Queen Victoria, England was visited by a very large number of American and Continental thieves, many of whom made their way to Manchester, attracted thither by the Exhibition. These "gentlemen" not only plied their trade at Old Trafford, but at the various banks and hotels in the city.

On the 19th July, 1887, I was in the Detective Office, when a cashier from the Manchester and Liverpool District Bank came in and related a very suspicious circumstance that had just taken place at that establishment. He stated that while a depositor was engaged in filling up a deposit note, having a large amount of money in gold, notes, and cheques on the counter before him, he was addressed by a stranger, who seemed to be busily engaged in filling up a paying-in form on his left. On turning his head to see what the man required, he noticed another individual, who was standing on his right, extract a fifty pound note from the money on the counter and leave a five pound note in its place.

"Here," said the depositor, "you have got the wrong note; you have picked up one of mine."

"Oh!" was the speedy reply, "I beg your pardon. Where shall I get the change for this note?"

The answer, the apology, and the inquiry, came so quickly and naturally, that the depositor thought that some mistake might possibly have been made, and took no further notice then of the matter. He went to the pay-in counter, and to the clerk there engaged related his adventure.

As the two men - one of whom was still busy pretending to fill in a form - appeared to be strangers, the clerk's suspicion was aroused, and he quickly communicated with the manager, who ordered the information to be at once conveyed to the Detective Office.

As the Exhibition and the Summer Assizes were both proceeding at the time, the Detective Office was left very bare of officers - in fact I was the only one available, having been left at headquarters by the Chief Constable.

I saw, however, that the chance was too good to let slip, so I accompanied the gentleman on whom the attempt had been made to endeavour to find the two men. The first bank to which we went was the Manchester and Liverpool District Branch Bank in King Street, but the suspect was not there, so we called in at the Manchester and County Bank in the same street. As we entered the porch I noticed a man with a lighted cigar in his fingers. He appeared to be paying about as much attention to an examination of the swing door as a cat generally does to a mouse-hole.

"Ah!" thought I, "the stop immediately!" The duty of this gentleman when his confederate has succeeded in effecting a robbery inside the bank, and got through the door, was to take the handle in his hand, and, under the pretence of passing through, to block the progress of anyone who might attempt to follow.

These bank thieves are also provided with large envelopes, ready directed, so that, if any alarm is given, after they succeed in getting outside with the plunder they put the notes into the envelopes and post them at the earliest opportunity. By this means, if they are apprehended, nothing is found upon them, and thus their identity is difficult to prove. Consequently great precaution is necessary lest there might be an action for illegal arrest.

On seeing this well-dressed individual paying such attention to the door, I turned to the gentleman who was with me and asked him as he passed through the door to take a good look at the man for the purpose of identifying him. He, however, failed to recognise him as one of the men who had been to the Manchester and Liverpool District Bank. So we went into the bank.

Amongst the crowd I noticed two men who were looking about without, apparently, having any legitimate business. The gentlemen failed, however, to recognise either of them. I watched them leave the bank and go along King Street separately. I directed the gentleman who accompanied me to look through the glass panel of a door, and he then thought one of them was the person who had picked up his note; but as I had the greatest difficulty in keeping him out of sight, I was at length compelled to let him go and use my own discretion.

I followed and saw that the three men were working in concert. They visited several banks, including the Joint Stock Bank, The Consolidated, the Lancashire and Yorkshire, Brooks's, the Manchester and County, and ultimately the Bank of England. One went into the bank, and as a police officer turned the corner of Pall Mall at that moment, I took hold of one of the others and handed him over to the officer. I then followed his companion into the bank, and as he was leaving I took him into custody, when he at once began to dispute the arrest by a display of physical force, which had to be subdued. After conveying the two to the Detective Office I went in search of their companion, but he had disappeared and was nowhere to be found. I then went to the Queen's Hotel, and found that they had been staying there for a few days, having arrived late one evening, as they said, from London.

One of the people connected with the hotel identified them, but they refused to give any account of themselves, and we were unable to make anything out of their antecedents. Their claim, however, to see the American Consul was loud and persistent. This gentleman was quite deceived by them, and up to their trial he expressed himself as believing them to be respectable people. At this point, a very unfortunate circumstance for the accused turned up. We began to trace to these "respectable" American citizens, a robbery of £140 from the counter of a bank in Liverpool, accomplished much in the same manner as the attempt made in the case of the Manchester Bank. The gentleman who had been robbed, however, was not quite sure as to the identification of the men, so as a little bounce I let it fall that I had some knowledge of the Liverpool robbery, which seemed to make them very uneasy.

Then complaints reached us of a similar bank robbery in London, and as the prisoners were told that they answered the description given, and that someone would shortly be over to identify them, it did not tend to make them more comfortable.

Ultimately they were committed by the Stipendiary Magistrate for trial at the Sessions, where one was sentenced to eight, and the other to nine months' imprisonment.

When taken into custody and searched, a considerable sum of money was found in the possession of each of these men, and sewn in the seam of the trousers worn by one, was a £50 note. Trace was afterwards obtained of the luggage of these gentlemen, and in a leather dressing case was found about £90 in notes, folded up and pushed in with a brush, a number of gold watches and chains, a number of diamond studs, all kinds of jewellery, and a full set of watchmaker's implements, together with a set of burglars' tools for opening safes, including alderman, punches, wedges, lead caps (to prevent sound when working at a safe), drills etc. There were also three revolvers, and a box of cartridges. The jewellery was in no doubt the proceeds of some safe robbery. The money was handed over to the solicitor for the defence, but the rest of the articles were detained, though many claims were made through him for the property. Whilst they were in prison, however, a photograph of each was sent to the United States, and the following record of crime was returned:-

George Goodwin *alias* William Stetson, Bill Snow, Bill Howard, and Bill the Brute, Trade Estate Agent; address refused. 1880, Hoboken, Jersey, U.S.A., Post-Office robbery, did not surrender to bail; 1881, Philadelphia, robbery, 3 years' imprisonment; 1887, August 7th, Manchester Sessions, 9 months.

William Brown, *alias* Roberts, Watson, Wylie's Kid, Big Bill, Commercial Traveller; address refused. 1880, New York: burglary, 6 months; 1882, burglary, acquitted; 1885, robbery, 2 years. August 7th, 1887, Manchester Sessions, 8 months.

After a time the American Consul was changed in Manchester, and several requests were made through him for the burglars' tools, and other property in the possession of the police; but this novel claim was not successful.

7

THE COUNTRY BUMPKIN AND HIS £200

I n March, 1884, Mr. J__ R __, a Cheshire farmer, was returning from the market when he was accosted in Market Street, Manchester, by a man who made some inquiries respecting a Stretford train. After answering these the man invited him to have a drink, after which they went into a public house, where they were joined by a third man. In the course of conversation the farmer happened to mention the part of Cheshire to which he belonged, when the last comer said that his father had lately died and left a large amount of money, £400 of which was to be distributed among the poor and needy of Cheshire. He proposed to give each of his companions £200 to distribute, with £20 each for their trouble, on condition that they each provided securities to show that they were worth this amount. R__, no doubt exhilarated at the idea of being of such service to his poorer brethren, besides having the chance of earning the bounty, accepted the offer, as also did his first acquaintance, and it was arranged that they would meet the following day at a public house in the neighbourhood of Oxford Road, and there produce the securities.

They assembled at the appointed time, when R___'s first acquaintance showed his securities to the stranger, and these proving satisfactory, R___ produced his own, consisting of two £100 Bank of England notes, which had been deposited in an envelope. Whilst the stranger was taking the notes from the envelopes to examine them, R___'s first acquaintance took off his hat, as if to wipe the perspiration from his brow, but held it in such a manner before R___'s face that he could not see what the stranger was doing. The latter, however, was busy transferring the notes from R___'s envelope to his own pocket book, and having substituted two leaves of a penny "Bradshaw's Railway Guide," returned the envelope to R___. The countryman now turned aside to examine the envelope and see that his notes were right, and whilst thus engaged the two "sharpers" made off, and getting into a passing hansom were soon lost to sight.

One of the notes a few minutes afterwards found its way into the Bank of England, where it was cashed for notes and gold, and a description of the men, with the numbers of the notes, was immediately put into circulation.

The description of one of the men, who wore a long beard and had signed his name on the back of the cashed note as "Henry Johnson," resembled that of a man I had previously arrested along with another for "ringing the changes," for which offence they had each been sentenced to nine months' imprisonment. On his release he had signed his name "Henry Johnson" in the police book, on receiving back the property taken from him on his arrest. Comparing the signature with that on the back of the note, I found the two to be in the same handwriting. My next task was to search for "Johnson;" but although his usual haunts were watched, no clue to his whereabouts could be found. I managed, however, to trace some of the notes, one having been cashed at a London tradesman's for a suit of clothes, and shortly afterwards the other £100 note was traced through the bank to a café keeper in Boulogne, who was a well-known "fence," or receiver of stolen property, and whose house was frequented by English and French railway and steamboat thieves. Some time later than this I saw "Johnson" in Manchester, but his whiskers, which had previously been about twelve inches long, giving him a very gentleman-like appearance, had been shaved off. This made such a difference in his looks that I was rather amazed, and was afraid that if I took him then there would be some difficulty in getting him identified. I therefore determined to keep my eye upon him, waiting until his beard had grown again.

In the meantime I interviewed the farmer, the cashier at the bank who had cashed the note, the barmaid of the public house, and two other persons who had seen the three men together. I found that the case was too strong even for this London "sharp" to set up an *alibi*.

One evening about half-past five, after resolving to arrest "Johnson," I was passing along Oak Street, and, nearing the Old Fleece Inn, a house noted as the haunt of thieves, I noticed that a fight was taking place outside, arising, no doubt, out of one of the usual "allocations" of its frequenters. As soon as I was noticed a general stampede took place, and Mr. "Johnson" and another flew up the street as fast as their legs could carry them. I gave chase and coming up alongside "Johnson" took hold of him. We walked along together for a short distance, when he suddenly turned round at the corner of a narrow street, and having given me a violent blow which made me reel, took once more to his heels. I managed, however, to keep my feet, and again coming up with him, seized him by the neck and dragged him into a cheese factor's shop, where I detained him until I received assistance. He was then removed to the Detective Office.

When the witnesses were taken to identify him, he tried every means in his power to deceive them; first putting on a muffler, then taking it off, putting on and taking off his overcoat, changing his hat, etc. But it was all useless. He was clearly identified, committed for trial at the Assizes, found guilty, and sentenced to ten years' penal servitude.

As for the old farmer - who made a practice of hiding his money in the chimney for fear of thieves, not daring to trust it to banks lest they might fail - nothing grieved him so much as to think he had taken £200 out of his hoard to entrust it to such a rogue as "Johnson."

8

BANK NOTE FORGERS

For some years we were in Manchester constantly receiving reports from various parts of the country respecting the uttering of forged bank notes, and in some cases large rewards were offered for private information which would lead to the apprehension and conviction of the forgers.

At this time we had in Manchester a man named John T__, who was known as "Johnny the Lawyer" among the "crooks" (thieves), from the fact that he was always posted up in law, and kept at his house "Stone's Justices' Manual," and other works on criminal jurisprudence. Whenever any swell thief fell into the clutches of the law, "Johnny" was waited upon by the thief's friends, and he gave them advice as to the particular line of defence which should be pursued.

We had also in Manchester at that period two men who were carrying on business as shopkeepers. One of them had served fourteen years' penal servitude for forgery, and the other, who had a residence in the country, and had been Clerk to the Chief of Police in a neighbouring borough, had previously been sentenced to five years' penal servitude for forgery, and two months' imprisonment at Sheffield Sessions for receiving stolen property. He was afterwards concerned in the great Leipsic frauds of 1887, in which, for obtaining £2,000 by means of a forged letter of credit, he was sentenced to five years' penal servitude, and ordered to pay a fine of three hundred marks, or in default four hundred days' extra imprisonment. This man went by the name of "Big Jim."

One day information arrived that a forged cheque had been uttered at one of the Manchester Banks, upon which £80 had been obtained. A description of the two men who had been concerned in the matter was handed in, and it was at once seen that "Big Jim" was one of the persons referred to. He was watched for and at last apprehended. When at the Detective Office he admitted that he was one of the men, and said, "A gentleman asked me the way to ___ Bank, and having nothing to do I took him there and waited until he got his money, for which he gave me the price of a drink. I had nothing to do with either the forgery or the uttering of the cheque." As his statement could not be controverted, he was discharged, and many a hearty laugh he and I have had since over the affair. He used to tell me that if he could pick up a couple of thousands "he would not trouble me any more."

One day, as I was visiting a suburb of Manchester, I saw from a tram-car window "Johnny the Lawyer." "Bottle Wilson," "Charlie the Barman," "Jack the Carpenter," and a person who went by the cognomen of "Starve." I got out of the car, and following them saw them enter a public house in Harpurhey. About an hour after, from the bedroom window of a shop opposite, which the occupant had kindly placed at my service, I saw "Jack" and "Starve" come out and take the tram. "Bottle" and "Charlie" followed in the next tram, and "Johnny the Lawyer" went to his house in ___.

I noticed that the last-mentioned was somewhat disguised; he had shaved his chin, and was wearing his whiskers in the "Lord Dundreary" style. I felt sure that their hour's chat had not been fruitless, and knowing them to be a very dangerous gang, I determined to keep my eye upon them - the more so as I had received many offers of a good reward if I could bring them to justice; for every few months they played sad havoc amongst the mercantile community in various parts of the country.

About a month later I received from Mr. Malcolm Wood, the Chief Constable - who knew I had been watching this gang for four years - a private communication which had been sent to him from the Chief Constable of Wakefield, asking if anything could be done to throw light on forged notes which were being circulated in that neighbourhood. On the 4th of December, 1883, the following circular was issued from Wakefield:

"Borough Police Office,
"Wakefield, Dec. 16th, 1883

"*Re Forged Bank Notes.*

"Sir,-

"Attached above I beg to hand you photographs of specimens of signatures endorsed on the backs of the forged notes uttered at Hull on the 30th ult., and at Huddersfield and Bradford on the 1st and 2nd inst.

"In all the known utterings the same two men appear to have taken part, either individually or together. The one described as the tall man is about thirty-eight years of age, fully five feet eleven inches high, slender figure, dark or black hair, whiskers and moustache, small space shaved on and under the chin, whiskers not bushy but rather wiry and straggling, dark piercing eyes; speaks rather slowly and correctly. Dress dark, tight-fitting overcoat, dark trousers, silk hat, dark scarf, with breast-pin, and black kid gloves, one of which he left in a shop where a note was changed, and which are rather a small size for so tall a man. He is, no doubt, a frequenter of race meetings, gambling houses, etc., and an associate of thieves and forgers. He was accompanied by a tall, stout, good-looking woman, dark hair and fresh complexion, dressed in dark ulster and black hat with feathers; had several rings on her fingers and wore earrings.

"The second man is described as short and stout, about thirty-five years of age, five feet five inches high, fresh complexion, light brown hair cut short, whiskers and moustache, clean shaven on chin and well up the sides of his face, thick necked, rather prominent eyes, corpulent, and looks 'horsey.' Dress - short drab top-coat, light trousers, and black billy-cock hat.

"Their *modus operandi* is for one of them to enter a shop and purchase an article of more or less value and tender in payment one of the forged notes, receiving the change in cash.

"As they will probably launch some new scheme of forgery, as they have no doubt done others before this, I am naturally very anxious that no effort should be spared to effect the arrest of these men.

"Would you, therefore, be kind enough to minutely compare the above with any signatures or handwriting you may have of persons you have had in custody at any time, and favour me with the result at your early convenience?

"Your obedient servant,
"(Signed) CHAS. T. CLARKSON,
"Chief Constable."

Upon the receipt of this communication I began to look the gang up again, but could find no trace whatever of them. Newspaper reports kept appearing of forged notes, and it was ascertained that some £800 worth of these were in circulation. Photographs of the endorsements upon them had been sent round to various towns, but were returned as "not recognised." In the meantime I kept my eyes open; and though I now and then saw one or another of the suspected men in Manchester, I could never drop upon two of them together. After some conversation with the Chief Constable it was decided that I should not act until such time as I could find them together.

One day, having an hour to spare, I sauntered in the direction of the house of "Johnny the Lawyer" to see what news I could gather, and on my way who should I drop across but "Johnny" himself. I could see that he was ill at ease, for his "Dundreary" whiskers had disappeared, and he would have avoided me if possible. I thought the best plan would be to appear unconcerned, not to give the slightest hint that I knew anything about the forgeries, and to try to worm myself into the confidence of "Johnny" to such an extent as to entirely deceive him as to my motive, with a view of thus inducing him to recall his "pals" to their old haunts, which I thought he might do if he got it into his head that they were safe in Manchester, for I had little doubt in my own mind that these were the gang who were doing all the mischief.

"Well, Johnny," I commenced, "I hear you have had a bad bout of sickness and been laid up at home." This was, of course, only a ruse on my part, but "Johnny" replied, "Yes; I have not been very well."

"I suppose that accounts for you not having been down town latterly. I hear that the fever has been rather prevalent in this quarter. You see the foundation on which this property is built is purely refuse, and it is not considered healthy. I suppose the fever has been busy in your family, for I see you have had your whiskers and hair shaved off. I hope, however, you will soon be well."

Having said this I made off without giving "Johnny" time to reply. The bait evidently took, for after this I could see him about daily in town, but there were no signs of any of his pals joining him. As I appeared to get no further I put a "plant" on his house, and another on that of "Charlie the Barman," keeping watch over the houses of the other three myself. "Starve" and "Jack the Carpenter" I never saw in town again. But after some months' close observation, during which "Johnny the Lawyer" kept going backwards and forwards, I received a communication on Sunday, 27th August, 1881, that he was in town. Going to the man who had kept observation on "Charlie the Barman's" old haunt, I ascertained that this gentleman had at last arrived in town. I then went to "Bottle's" house, and saw him through the window in company with two men who had lately arrived from Australia, and whom I knew to be noted thieves.

About half-past eleven the same night I started for the house of "Charlie the Barman," in Upper Moss Lane, and after watching a while saw the shadow of his figure on the window blind in the room over the shop. I obtained admittance, arrested him, and sent him to the Police Station in charge of two officers. I then went to "Bottle's" house in Denmark Road, and placing two officers at the back, directed another in uniform to go to the front door, and to say that "he had been sent by 'Charlie' to ask 'Bottle' to come to the Police Office and bail him out." "Bottle" declined the invitation, and made an attempt to escape by the back. On seeing the officers he turned into the house again, and the uniform officer was told that he was not in. I had been watching from a garden on the opposite side of the street, and on the uniform officer leaving the door, I advanced towards it; as I did so the door was opened and "Bottle" was preparing for a run, but catching a glimpse of me he closed the door with a bang and ran down the lobby. I threatened to burst the door in if they did not open it. After some time my request was complied with, and I entered the house. I found "Bottle" in the kitchen, and after a good deal of parleying on his part, I got him to the Detective Office.

It was now 3 a.m., but I drove to the house of "Johnny the Lawyer," and after knocking him up told him that I had come to take him into custody. "Where's your warrant?" he roared. "I have none. I am taking you on suspicion of being concerned in some forgery frauds," was my answer. "Well, we'll see about this suspicion," he replied, defiantly. On the way to the Police Station I heard him say to the officers to whom he was handcuffed, "I saw him up here some time ago. I thought then he was on for something. He has been waiting, and I expect some surprise is in store for me."

The look of amazement that came over "Johnny's" face when I called the other two confederates out of a cell at the Station, and asked if they would like to be placed together, could never be forgotten by those who witnessed it.

They elected to be placed together, though they denied that they were known to each other. They were afterwards identified by witnesses from Hull, York, and Scarborough, and being taken first to Wakefield, and thence to Hull, were committed for trial at York Assizes.

They were defended by Mr. Lockwood, Q.C., and Mr. Blackburn; Mr. Tyndall Atkinson, Q.C., and Mr. Wortley prosecuting. All there were found guilty on November 2nd, 1881, and the "Lawyer" was sentenced to seven years', the "Barman" to ten years', and "Bottle" to fourteen years' penal servitude.

When before the magistrates at Wakefield Police Court the prosecuting solicitor in saying that he had made out a *prima facie* case used the phrase several times, whereupon "Johnny the Lawyer," leaning over the dock, coolly remarked to the solicitor for the defence, "There's a good deal of *prima facie* about it. What will he say when he comes to the substance?"

After their conviction I received rewards from Messrs. Woodall, of Scarborough, and Messrs. Latham, Tew & Co., of Wakefield.

After "Johnny's" release I saw him one day at Victoria Station, London, and knowing that he had no business there without reporting himself, I telegraphed to Manchester and asked my colleagues to visit "Johnny's" house, my intention being to arrest him at the end of the forty-eight hours for being absent from home without reporting himself as he was required to do by law; but "Johnny" was one too many for me this time. He had seen me in London, and had taken the very next train to Manchester. When the officer called at his home, he politely opened the door and invited him inside, telling him at the same time to give his compliments to Caminada.

I had him again soon afterwards, however, on a charge of stealing from the person, for which he and two others were each sentenced, at the Llangollen Sessions on January 4th, 1888, to seven years' penal servitude; while a fourth prisoner with them was committed for twelve months. "Johnny" evidently expected a much longer sentence, for on our way to the prison he remarked, "There's nothing for it now but wishing the old woman dead." Thinking that he referred to his mother, I asked why, when he soon undeceived me with the answer, "Oh! When the son and heir comes to the throne he may let some of us fellows loose."

"Johnny's" previous convictions were: - 1864, Edinburgh, thirty-two days for pocket picking; 1868, Manchester, three months' for pocket picking; 1869, Manchester, twelve months' for larceny. "Bottle" had served five years' penal servitude, and the "Barman" twelve months' and other terms of imprisonment.

9

THE CONFIDENCE TRICK

THE THREE "HONESTEST" MEN IN THE WORLD

Few cities in the world have within them so many thieves as Manchester. The pavement of Cottonopolis is incessantly trodden by rogues. This is not surprising. The facility afforded for hiding in a crowd induces those who are badly disposed to resort hither from all parts of the globe.

A great number of these persons are fixed constantly in this great City. Some come only like birds of passage - at the approach of great occasions, or during the racing or other busy seasons.

Among those permanently located in the City are a class of thieves of incredible effrontery, who work what is called the "confidence trick."

Some years ago a young man living in Lincolnshire took advantage of one of the summer excursions to that well-known place of entertainment - Belle Vue Gardens - intending at the same time to visit his uncle who resided in the City. On his arrival at London Road Railway Station he was accosted with an inquiry as to whether he came from Louth, by a sharper who was on the look-out for a suitable

victim among the "country Johnnies." The bow thus drawn
at a venture scarcely hit the mark, as the young man came
from Conisboro'; but it served the purpose of opening a
conversation, and the two walked along together. The usual
invitation to "have a glass" was given, and an adjournment
to a public house followed. Here they were joined by a third
man, and in course of conversation it was suggested that the
first "sharper" was on the look-out for someone who would
distribute in Lincolnshire a large sum of money which was
to be given to a public charity, or to the poor of that county.

After various modes of distribution had been discussed,
it was only natural that the conversation should turn upon
the honesty of the persons who have to be trusted.

Sharper No. 1 was a very confiding man. He was charitable not only in money matters, but had much of the
charity of which St. Paul speaketh; he had great confidence
in the honesty of his fellow creatures. To prove this he
proposed to give his purse into the possession of the
"stranger" who had last joined them.

He would allow him to walk out of the house for five
minutes, after which time he was to return and prove that
he was an honest man, or to be ever afterwards branded
with dishonesty. The stranger, nothing loath to prove his
honesty, accepted the invitation, and sailed forth with the
purse, returning at the end of the stipulated time, thus
proving himself an honest man, and satisfactorily establishing that there was something in the theory of the
"benevolent gentleman," who insisted that all men were not
rogues. The stranger, it was hinted, ought now to try the
honesty of the charitable gentleman, which he did by
entrusting him with his purse whilst he went through the
same performance. It is surely needless to say that such a

benefactor to his race proved himself eminently trustworthy.

Now up went a chorus of approval. Could three honester men be found in the world? But, ah! there was one little defect. The confidence of the Lincolnshire excursionist had not yet been tried! This was the time to prove his faith in the honesty of his companions. Ashamed to be doubted in such excellent company, the visitor put his purse, containing seven pounds twelve shillings, into the hands of his first acquaintance, who went for the usual walk; but as he stayed rather over the stipulated time, the "stranger" became uneasy, and began to look around for his "friends."

Noticing his trouble the barman asked what was the matter, whereupon the story was told. The barman advised him to waste no time, but to seek his uncle and report the matter to the police. When the uncle heard the story, he took him to the railway station, paid his fare, and sent him back to Conisboro' a sadder, but, let us hope, a wiser man.

This is only one of the many cases of this kind which I have come across during my career. If it were not for the hard facts established over and over again, it would be almost incredible that full-grown men should be found ready to become the dupes of those who so successfully practice the "confidence trick."

10

RINGING THE CHANGES; OR, THE "BUSTLE"

This is a class of theft which differs from all others, in that it requires a good deal of boldness and self-possession. Thieves who "ring the changes" usually work in couples, and the place selected for their operations are those which are busiest. Two of these people enter a place of business at an appropriate moment. One of them orders something and tenders a sovereign in payment. No sooner does he get the change than the other in a hurry says, "Oh! I have got less change than that, I'll pay," and at the same moment presents half-a-sovereign. "Very well," replies the first; "give me my sovereign back." Then when the person supplying the goods gets the half sovereign, the purchaser finds that he has got a shilling, and the half sovereign is asked for back, and the shilling is given in its place.

The object is to "bustle" the person who is supplying the goods, and the dodge invariably succeeds, the purchasers getting hold of their own sovereign, the change for the sovereign, the change for the half sovereign, and the change for the shilling; while the person serving them seldom finds out the mistake until going to the till for change, when the "sharps" have, of course, flown. Should the mistake be discovered before they can get away, or if the tradesman or servant be too sharp for them, it is always easy to confess to a mistake.

About the year 1884 there were many complaints from business people in various parts of Manchester regarding this sort of fraud. From the description given it appeared that two men were engaged in these transactions, one described as a very easy-going fellow, a slow talker, and the other a man of gentleman-like appearance who, in almost every case, produced from his coat pocket patterns of cloth at which his companion looked.

At the time we had in Manchester two men who were a mystery to me. I could neither ascertain what they did nor where they lived. Complaints continued to roll in, and after between thirty or forty had been received - sometimes as many as five in one day, the complainants in many cases declining to prosecute - I made up my mind to tackle these mysterious strangers on the subject.

One day passing along City Road I saw the younger of the two coming in an opposite direction, and as we met face to face I accosted him with, "Good morning. How are you?" There was no reply, so I continued, "I am a detective officer, and as I believe you are a man who is wanted for an offence, I must request you to accompany me to the Detective Office."

Of course, the usual pains and penalties were threatened if I attempted to put my hands on him, but I gave him clearly to understand that I was not to be bounced out of the matter, and succeeded in getting him to the Detective Office where he was identified. He declined to give any address on the ground that it would disgrace his family, and that it was a case of mistaken identity which could soon be set right. On searching him I found his pattern book and a number of business cards in his possession, inscribed as follows:-

"Cloth manufacturer and Commission Agent for the Colonies."

The difficulty now was to get hold of the slow-speaking gentleman. I had seen him several times get off the Stretford tram-car, and I learned from one of the old drivers who saw me noticing him, and who appeared to pay as much attention to him as I did, that he had observed him going into some new property off King Street, Stretford.

On the following morning I went to the place named, and after about half-an-hour's inquiry found that my man of mystery was also a mystery in the neighbourhood in which he lived. All that was known about him was that he called himself a "dealer in antiquities." I took him to town where he was identified. He and his companions were committed and tried at the Sessions on seven cases, and were each sentenced to nine months' imprisonment.

11

AN ARMED BURGLAR

Robert Horridge (he was more familiarly called "Bob" Horridge), who forms the subject of this story, was born in Rochdale Road, Manchester, in the year 1849, of very respectable and industrious parents. When a boy he was sent to St. Paul's School, Rochdale Road, and he had also to assist his father in his business as smith and maker of fenders. When "Bob" was quite young he showed signs of unusual depravity. These speedily developed, as a result most probably of bad companions, and at the age of thirteen years he was sentenced to six months' imprisonment.

On his release from gaol he again went to work with his father, and for a time behaved exceedingly well. He appeared to have given up his evil habits, but was again apprehended and sentenced to eighteen months' imprisonment. At the expiration of this further term of imprisonment, he resumed work for his father, and by his industry managed to save sufficient money to start business on his own account. He took into partnership an Italian - a steady and industrious man - who worked for one of the telegraph companies which existed before the telegraphs were acquired by the Government.

During the year 1869, we received at the Manchester Detective Office a large number of complaints of errand boys, sent out by tradesmen with parcels, being met by a man who asked if the parcel was for Mr. or Mrs.___, having by some means or other ascertained the name and address of the person to whom the parcel was consigned. On receiving a reply in the affirmative, he said he had been instructed to call for the parcel and take it with him. The parcels were invariably given up, but, needless to say, they never reached their proper destination. For a long time no clue could be obtained to the offender nor to the parcels, until one day a youngster who had been persuaded to part with a parcel in this way, immediately afterwards regretted having done so, and cried out, "He's stole my parcel." That cry was taken up by another boy, and the thief was caught. The culprit, "Ned" by name, was a well known pal of "Bob's," and was in his company on every possible occasion.

After inquiring, it was ascertained that "Ned" had many times been observed going to "Bob's" house with brown paper parcels - always very hurriedly - and been seen to leave equally quickly without the parcels. It was therefore decided to overhaul "Bob's" house. I was taken by one of our Inspectors to assist in the search, and this was my first introduction to Mr Horridge.

When we entered "Bob's" house, he became very sullen, and, learning our errand, threatened violence. This led me to seize him and force him into a corner of the room, where I kept him until the search was completed. We always knew each other afterwards, and whenever we met "Bob" would clench his teeth at me; but I always kept up a bold front to him, and never allowed him to think I was afraid of him.

Shortly after this affair, a man reported to the police that he had been robbed of his watch in close proximity to one of the railway stations in Manchester, and, thinking it was just possible that the theft had been witnessed by some of the shopkeepers in the neighbourhood, a watchmaker who lived hard by was spoken to, and the watch described to him. The face of the watch had, it appeared, on one occasion been opened with a knife, and the knife slipping had caused a piece of metal to be chipped off the dial. On the morning following the robbery, a colleague and I were passing the watchmaker's shop, when we saw "Bob" leave in front of us. My colleague immediately entered the shop and asked what "Bob" had been doing there? He had left a watch to be repaired. The watchmaker produced the watch, looked at us, and laughed, saying, "Why, it's the watch you spoke to me about, and he will call for it tomorrow morning." We compared the watch with the description given to us, and found it corresponded exactly.

We were at the shop early the next morning, and as soon as "Bob" came in for the watch we suddenly emerged from our place of concealment and took him into custody. When questioned, he said, "I bought it from a man I do not know." "You had better tell that to the magistrates; no doubt they will believe you," I answered. Soon afterwards the Italian partner, who had taken a receiver's share in the robbery, was arrested. Both were committed for trial, and at the Sessions were found guilty of stealing and receiving. Horridge, on account of his previous bad character, was sentenced to seven years' penal servitude, and the Italian to four months' imprisonment.

It was, however, only subsequently that "Bob's" real career of crime began. He was a smart, athletic fellow, and was always ready for a boxing bout. Men who had an intimate knowledge of him have told me that he was a first-class workman, and that a better man at his trade - the fire and anvil - could not be found, for he could do half as much work again as any other smith in the country.

On his release from penal servitude, "Bob" again went into business for himself in Style Street, Rochdale Road. He was very successful, and soon bought a pony and a long cart with low sides, which was necessary for him to convey his goods to the various wholesale houses with which he did business. It was very well known that when "Bob" was not in prison robberies occurred more frequently in Manchester than when he was confined. Every now and again, during his days of liberty, a safe in some secluded spot would be overturned, and the side or back cut out, and everything of value removed therefrom. First a furrier's shop was broken into, then a silk mercer's, and so on, the robberies occurring in rapid succession. One Sunday morning about six o'clock, a jeweller's shop in Bradshaw Street, Shudehill, was entered. A number of officers were out looking for Horridge's gang, but we could get no further than that he had been seen about 6.30 going in the direction of his house carrying a heavy hammer. This circumstance made it clear to us that "Bob" had had a hand in the robbery that morning. Shortly afterwards, he was suspected of a robbery in the county, and the police arrived from that district to try and effect his capture. We went to a house, in which he then was, in Gould Street. Between twenty and thirty officers surrounded the house, and a loud knock was given at the door. "Bob" jumped up and tapped at the window; broke his way through the laths and plaster of the ceiling, and was soon out on the roofs. Away over the slates he scampered, until he reached Ludgate Hill, an adjoining street, when through the roof he dashed. Making his way through the ceiling, he dropped into a bedroom in which a number of harvestmen were sleeping. They were naturally considerably startled at "Bob's" sudden and unsuspected entry, but they made no effort to detain him. "Bob" ran down the bedroom stairs, and on opening the front door, which was reached by four steps from the street, saw two constables ready to receive him. Without a moment's hesitation he took what I cannot otherwise describe as a flying-leap into the street, over the heads of the two officers. He dropped upon his feet, and, waving only his shirt and trousers, got safely away from all his pursuers.

"Bob's" next exploit was in a fancy goods shop in Thomas Street. The shutter of the shop was made with an aperture, for the purpose of giving the police a view of the interior. The policeman on the beat, looking through this aperture, saw "Bob" and a companion known as "Long Dick" busily at work in the shop. Each was wearing an apron, and one was reaching parcels down from the shelves while the other was examining them. On seeing the officer "Bob" cried out, "It's all right, guv'nor; we're taking stock!" The officer had only just come on his beat, and as it was his first visit, he went round to the back of the shop to see that all was safe. "Bob," who thought the officer had gone to the back for the purpose of apprehending them, made his way out, and meeting the officer in the passage, struck him a violent blow in the face, knocked him down, and made his own escape. The officer's call for help brought another constable to the scene, when "Long Dick" rushed out of the shop; but he was at once secured. He was forthwith taken before the court, and sentenced to five years' penal servitude.

"Bob" kept well out of the way during the trial. A few days afterwards, two detective-sergeants entered a house in

Addington Street, Oldham Road, where "Bob" was living. He was upstairs at the time, and must have seen them enter, for they had not been in the house long before he leaned over the bannisters and cried out, "Have they gone?" "No," said one of the officers; "we are here," running upstairs at the same time. "Bob" resorted to his usual tactics - jumped on the bed, through the manhole, along the ceiling, and dropped through into an adjoining house. He ran rapidly downstairs, and again made his escape. The officer who followed "Bob" over the rafters lost his watch and chain, damaged his clothes, and presented a sorry spectacle after the chase was over. "Bob" was not long before he was again at his old tricks, and his next escapade worthy of notice was at a mill at Bradford, near Manchester. It was usual at this mill to draw out of the bank on Friday the cash that was required to pay the wages on Saturday. "Bob's" tactics in this case showed the extent of the measures he was prepared to take in order to effect a robbery.

He first of all, in some way or other, learned the secret that a good deal of cash was in the safe on Friday night, and thus he selected the time for operation. His next observation was directed to the watchman, and he soon discovered that it was the practice of this peaceful guardian each morning about half-past four to leave the office by the mill door, and go round to the boiler-house in order to get up steam, so that work might be started by six o'clock. It was further noticed that, on Saturday morning, the watchman took the precaution to lock the front door and carry away the key in his pocket. Having thus discovered when and how he could best gain admission to the premises, "Bob" fitted a false key to the door, and thus all was ready for the visit. One Saturday morning, "Bob" and three of his companions drove in his cart to the neighbourhood of the mill. They

were later in reaching their destination than they antici-
pated, and the watchman was later than usual in leaving the
office. The consequence was that the cart was driven near
the mill, which was fronted by a croft, and when the
watchman turned out he noticed the group. "Bob" and one
of his companions immediately began to fight, or rather
pretended to fight; but by moral suasion on the part of the
others, assisted by the unsuspicious watchman, the quarrel
was made up. The "antagonists" parted good friends, and
the watchman proceeded to the boiler house to get up the
steam. The cart was then brought close up to the mill, the
office easily entered by means of the false key, and the safe,
weighing 450 lbs, containing about £600 in gold and silver,
taken away.

This was certainly a startling inquiry for the police to
enter upon. The papers teemed with accounts of a "Daring
Safe Robbery in Manchester," and people stared when they
heard that no arrest had been made. The daring and boldness of the robbery almost took people's breath away. One
could scarcely picture a watchman on the spot, a safe and its
contents stolen, and the thieves to get clear away! "Whatever
will happen next?" "Where are the police?" and "What are
the detectives doing?" were questions everybody asked. We
were, however, not long before we had "Bob's" gang "spot-
ted" for the "job," and the next thing was to get them identified. But this was a most difficult matter. The watchman
could not recognise them, and several others who saw them
were unable to swear to them. "Bob" had, it seemed, clearly
beaten us this time. But about a fortnight after the robbery
we got a "wrinkle" where the safe was to be found. "Bob's"
workshop consisted of three cellars under dwelling-houses,
and behind the workshop was a reservoir which supplied
with water an old mill adjoining. This reservoir had been

made the resting-place of the empty safe! It was in about 5ft. of water, and could not be seen from the surface. The millowner was induced to lower the water sufficiently to allow of lifting tackle being put round the safe, and it was hoisted out. An examination showed that everything had gone, the back of the safe having been cut completely away.

In the month of July, 1880, an officer in uniform was going his rounds, and on trying the door of a warehouse in Redfern Street found it was insecure. Pressing against it, it yielded a little. Pushing it again and again, it suddenly gave way, when out rushed "Bob." He struck the officer a violent blow which felled him, and made off at full speed along Redfern Street, Mayes Street, and Long Millgate. The constable soon regained his feet, and was in hot pursuit crying "Stop thief!" An officer in the distance heard the cry, and went straight for "Bob;" but it was of no use. He toppled over like a skittle under "Bob's" heavy blows, and a gentleman connected with one of the newspaper offices who essayed to capture "Bob" shared the same fate. Down the steps that once formed an approach to Victoria Station by the foot-bridge Horridge rushed, bounding over the parapet into the filthy Irk, dashed along the river into the tunnel running under the Grammar School, Walker's Croft, and Hunt's Bank, emerging at the junction of the waters into the River Irwell, until he came to a croft in Moreton Street, Strangeways, where he got clear away. "Bob" was thus once more a free man. In a few days he was seen again at work, and it was decided to try a fresh plan with him. An inspector went to his smithy, and, looking through the window, thus addressed him -

"Well, Bob, how are you?" Shall you be busy to-night?"

"No," replied Bob.

"Then," said the Inspector, "I should like to see you at the Prince's Feathers, at 7 o'clock, if it is convenient."

"Bob" swallowed the bait, singular as the fact may appear, and kept the appointment. As soon as he entered the place, two other officers walked in and invited "Bob" to accompany them to the Detective Office. There he was placed with a number of others, and was identified by both the police officers, and also by the civilian, from whom he had previously escaped. He was committed for trial, found guilty, and sentenced to 7 years' penal servitude, to be followed by 7 years' police supervision. This put a stop to his performances for a time. At this period it was customary to remove the prisoners a few weeks after conviction from the ordinary prisons to the convict establishment, and while "Bob" was being conveyed to London by rail, chained with about fifteen other convicts, he told his companions that it would not be long before he regained his liberty, or he would take care that there was a mutiny in the prison. This was overheard by the officer in charge, and he informed the Governor of the prison on his arrival so that the warders could be in readiness to prevent an escape. But "Bob" was as good as his word. He induced the convicts to agree to his plan; but when the signal was given, only two besides himself had the courage to attempt it. An alarm was raised, the guard turned out, and called upon the prisoners to stand. Two of them threw up their arms as an intimation of surrender, but "Bob" continued his flight. The guard fired and wounded him, but still he went on. Again they fired and hit him, but the runaway was gifted with more determination than most men, and, in spite of his wounds, he continued his flight. A third time the guard discharged his carbine, and "Bob" was then compelled to surrender. He was marched back to prison, and very carefully watched until the day of his liberation arrived in April, 1887.

One of the first things he did on coming out of prison was to inquire the whereabouts of his two companions who had shown the "white feather" when the attempt to escape was made, and he would be revenged, he said, for their cowardice.

His next exploit was to break into the shop of Mr. Angus Wood, in Rochdale Road, by means of false keys. This time he was assisted by a woman. They were surprised about 4.30 a.m. by the officer on beat, who summoned to his assistance a letter carrier and two other persons, one of whom, assisted by the letter carrier, watched the side door of the shop. "Bob" unbolted the back door of the shop and let himself into the yard behind, saying as he did so, "I will not be taken alive." As soon as he opened the yard door he discharged a revolver at the constable's head. The bullet scarred his neck sharply, and dazed him. "Bob" and the officer's assistants all took to flight by different routes. Another officer met "Bob" in his flight and endeavoured to stop him, but the desperado fired again and shot the officer in the breast, causing him to stagger and fall. "Bob" then once more got clear away. The wounded constable was taken in a passing market cart to the Infirmary, where he remained for about three weeks, and I may safely say that he will never be right again.

On it becoming known that two police officers had been shot at, and that the would-be murderer remained at large, no little uneasiness was caused in the minds of the public, who probably feared he would pay some of them a visit.

I was at this time at Chichester on other business, and there I received a telegram informing me of the occurrence and requesting my immediate return to headquarters. I reached Manchester about 5.30 in the afternoon and at once set to work to make inquiries, and soon ascertained that "Bob" was the man wanted for the attempted murder and the robbery. I was cautioned by "Bob's" father and sister to be very careful what I was doing, as, since his discharge from Parkhurst on the 5th of April, 1887, they had often heard him say he would shoot *me*. This, certainly, was very pleasant news; but, knowing the desperate character of the man, I was not surprised to hear it. I traced "Bob" to the house of a relative at Moss Side, and from there in turn to Ardwick, Stockport, and Tiviot Dale, where I learned he had taken the train for Liverpool. I instructed officers to watch the house in Manchester where he lived - his wife being away at this time - and also to watch the house of a friend of his wife's. Then, with other members of the detective staff, I went to Liverpool and made a close search for "Bob." While we were in Liverpool his wife was taken into custody at Manchester, to which place we returned, when she stated she had left her husband in Bolton.

At night we went to the latter town, and walked about with her until three o'clock the next morning, when she laid down on the flags and fell sound asleep. She was the only clue we had, and it was necessary to watch her keenly to prevent her getting away.

On the following evening, whilst observing her house, I saw her leave with a mantle over her head, hail a cab and drive to Knott Mill Station, the ascent to which is by two flights of steps, so that it would be easy for her to ascertain if she was followed by turning her head. After a short time I entered the station, and learned that she had booked to Liverpool by the South Junction line. I hurried to the Central Station and took a train for the same place. It was during the strike of the railway men, and my arrival was half-an-hour later than that of "Bob's" wife, or "Little Ada" as she was called. We searched all night, and saw Ada leave Liverpool on the following evening. We kept up our disguise, and went to the neighbourhood of the docks to search for "Bob" there. In walking along Duke Street, I saw one of my colleagues enter the "Prince of Wales" public house, and a little further on another colleague came up to me and said, "Did you see that man who has just passed?" "Yes!" I replied. He answered, "I saw him look very hard at you." I turned round to get a better view, and at once recognised "Bob" by his walk. "It's him!" I exclaimed. "Bob" was just crossing Duke Street, and was apparently about to enter the "Prince of Wales" public house. Stooping down I ran up to "Bob" and seized him by the arms. "Hallo! Bob, how are you?" I asked. He quickly put his hand towards his pocket, when I drew a revolver and, placing the muzzle to his mouth with the weapon at full cock, said, "If there's any nonsense with you, you'll get the contents of this." "Bob's" experience of our first meeting twenty years before caused him to think there was trouble in store for him, and again he tried to get his hand to his pocket. I shouted to Inspector Schofield, who was near, "Double up, Will," and he ran to my assistance. "Bob's" arms were firmly held. He refused to walk, and, as we were dragging him along to the nearest police station, he made a desperate effort to free himself, saying, as he did so, "I have nothing," trying to make us believe he was not armed. I struck him on the head with my revolver, and said, "Perhaps you'll come quietly now." In Bold Street we met a policeman in uniform who gladly assisted us, remarking, when told who the prisoner was, "He might have killed a dozen police officers if he had not been apprehended."

"I have nothing," again protested "Bob" at the Detective Office; but I knew he only wanted an opportunity to shoot both of us. Directing Schofield to hold one of his hands, and having myself secured the other, I was about to search him. Seeing that he could not deceive me, he sullenly exclaimed, "It's in there." Thrusting my hand into his trouser's pocket, I pulled out a six-chambered revolver, fully loaded, together with a small tin box containing some loose cartridges. Sergeant Standen was the officer who entered the "Prince of Wales" public house, and he did not know we had made the arrest until I returned in a cab to Duke Street.

In was in the neighbourhood that we had seen "Little Ada" cross to the Central Station, and this was the only quarter of Liverpool which we had not explored. While searching that city for "Bob," I determined to visit the house of a notorious Birmingham thief known as "Wingey," from the fact that he had lost the fingers of one hand. Inspector Robins, of the Liverpool detective police, accompanied me to the house. We were refused admission, and, on entering, a large bull dog confronted us in the lobby. Producing my revolver, I threatened to shoot it if the inmates did not take it away. They saw that I meant what I said, and wisely secured the brute, while we went over the place to satisfy ourselves that Horridge was not in hiding there.

"Bob" was conveyed to Manchester by the 11.30 p.m. train, and at the Detective Office he made a written statement in accordance with my depositions given below.

Next morning he was clearly identified when placed in the company of a number of other men. Before the Magistrates, he was charged with "having broken and entered the shop of Mr. Wood, and stolen six pairs of boots" (he had removed these boots from one place to another whilst he was in the shop). He was further charged with "having shot with a revolver, loaded with bullets, Police Constable Parkin, with intent and malice aforethought to kill and murder him;" and a similar charge was preferred against him in regard to Police Constable Bannon. He was committed for trial at the Assizes.

In view of the great public interest which the capture of Horridge created I append a copy of my deposition in the case, which was as follows:-

"Jerome Caminada, Chief Inspector of Police in this city, says: On the evening of the 8th of August last I was in Duke Street, Liverpool, between ten and eleven o'clock. I was looking for the male prisoner (Elizabeth Ann Stone was indicted with 'Bob'). Inspector Schofield and Sergeant Standen were with me, Schofield and I being armed. I have known Horridge for nineteen years. I was walking along the street alone. Standen was in a public-house, and Schofield a little distance away. The prisoner came along the street from the other direction. I passed him by and then turned back and got hold of him, putting my arms round his arms. I said, 'Hallo, Bob! How are you?' and shook him up. Schofield then came towards me. We were all dressed as labourers. He did not seem to recognise me at first, but put his arms down towards his pockets, and tried to get his hand into his right hand trousers pocket. I got hold of his arm to prevent his doing so. He said, 'What's it about? Loose my hands; I have got nothing about me.' I said, 'Now if there is any nonsense, Bob, we will settle it between us,' and I showed him my revolver. Schofield ran up and got hold of him, and we took him along Duke Street towards Great George Street. At the top of Duke Street he made a final effort to get loose, and I struck him on the head with my revolver. This made him half dazed, and as we dragged him along he said, 'I have had to do what I did, or they would have killed me; it was the officer's own fault he was shot - he would come on to it.' This was before I told him with what he would be charged, and was not in reply to any remark of mine. Up to then I had said nothing more than I have stated. I took him to the detective office, Dale Street, Liverpool, and there charged him with breaking and entering a boot shop, 633, Rochdale Road, Manchester, on the morning of the 30th of July, and stealing a quantity of boots value 40s., and told him that he would be further charged with attempting to murder Police-Constables Bannon and Parkin whilst in the execution of their duty by shooting them with a revolver. He said, 'I did not intend to kill them or hurt them - I only intended to frighten them.' I searched him and found on him in his right hand trousers pocket the six-chambered revolver produced, all the chambers being loaded, and also six other cartridges produced. When charged at Manchester, I repeated to the prisoner what he had said at Liverpool and it was written down. Prisoner said, 'I will plead guilty to all the charges you bring against me.' Inspector Schofield and Sergeant Standen were present and heard this.

In the meantime his pals had resolved to give him a last chance, subscribing among them the necessary sum, 23s. 6d., for a dock-brief.

At the close of the evidence for the prosecution the barrister who held the dock-brief rose with all the dignity which the grave nature of the proceedings demanded, and, pulling his gown over his shoulders and fixing his wig more firmly on his head, glared round the Court, and then at the opposing Counsel, as though ready if need be to defend by physical force the innocence of the prisoner. Turning his face to the gallery, and fixing his thumb in the arm-holes of his gown, the learned luminary of the law began his address in a stentorian voice. After referring to the heavy responsi-bility which rested upon his shoulders, he proceeded to air his eloquence to the gallery in one of those speeches so common on such occasions when there is no defence - that is, to blackguard the prosecution. After indulging in some high-flown, bombastic language, merely to tickle the vanity of his patrons, he concluded by appealing to the high-minded and intelligent jury to let the cause of truth and justice prevail by the acquittal of his much-injured and most oppressed client.

When the loquacious advocate sat down, the Judge in a few words demolished the whole fabric he had so diligently erected; and the high-minded and intelligent jury, ignoring his appeal without so much as leaving the box, found the prisoner guilty, the Judge sentencing him to penal servitude for life.

The following is a rough copy of "Bob's" convictions in Manchester:- 1862: Stealing money - 6 months' imprisonment; May, 1867: Receiving stolen property - 18 months' imprisonment; March, 1870: Stealing a watch - 7 years' penal servitude and 7 years' police supervision; August 4, 1880: Breaking into warehouse - 8 years' penal servitude and 7 years' police supervision; Nov. 2, 1887: Attempted murder and robbery - penal servitude for life.

In addition to the above sentences, Horridge made other appearances before the magistrates. On one occasion early in his career he was committed to gaol because he failed to find sureties for his good behaviour. Again, in August, 1876, he was tried for doing malicious damage by cutting the bellows of a rival smith, or "rattening" him. This offence could not, however, be clearly brought home to him. In October of the following year Horridge was indicted for shop-breaking, and his plea of not guilty again stood him in good stead, for his identity as the actual thief could not be positively established to the satisfaction of the jury.

When Horridge was sent into penal servitude for life the public had the pleasure of knowing that the career of one of the most accomplished and desperate thieves that ever lived in Manchester was brought to an end. "Bob" is at the present time confined in one of Her Majesty's convict prisons, and after his previous doings the greatest possible care is taken of him.

12

HOW I TRACKED TWO INCENDIARIES

A PLOT TO DEFRAUD AN INSURANCE COMPANY

In April, 1886, I received information of a rather suspicious circumstance relating to a shop in Chorlton Road, Hulme, in charge of a young lady. A nurse, who was engaged by the wife of a plumber who had met with an accident, alleged that whilst sitting up with that lady's husband she heard during the night certain noises in the next shop - a tobacconist's - after it had been closed. As no one was supposed to live on the premises referred to, I set to work to see how these noises could be explained. I called at the shop, ostensibly to purchase a box of cigars of a special brand and quality. After a little conversation I suggested that a splendid business might be done in the neighbourhood if a good and choice stock of cigars were kept. The young lady was of a communicative disposition, and I ascertained that one of her employers occasionally came to the shop and remained for some time after she had gone away, taking the key to her house on leaving. I endeavoured to make an appointment to meet her. She said she had to see her young gentleman, who worked in a shop near at hand, at half-past eight that night; but she promised to meet me an hour earlier when she left the shop. I took the precaution to have a lady assistant with me, and after a little persuasion we prevailed upon the shop assistant to take tea with us, which I had previously ordered for half-past seven. To guard against being seen with the young lady I walked on in front, the two ladies following. As the tea proceeded I learned that one of her employers was a builder; but she did not know the occupation of the other, who, however, often visited the place - always at night - when he generally walked right through the back portion of the premises without stopping or speaking to her. I also ascertained that she did not know what the back premises or the rooms above the shop contained, as the door was always locked, and every care taken to prevent her seeing inside. The partners had met there several times, and one of them had been working on the premises for several days; but she was told it was a private business and was cautioned against going upstairs. In answer to further questions she told me that the "takings" were about 6s. per week, that her salary was 8s. per week, and the rest of the shop 10s. per week.

After tea the young lady took her departure, and, with a promise from me of something handsome for her trouble, left the keys of the outer door in my charge. With these I gained admission to the shop, and by means of a pick-lock made a thorough search of the premises. The door of each room was securely locked. Blinds were hung at the windows of the front rooms, the window openings being covered up inside by thin boards, which were moveable, so that it was impossible for anyone to see from the outside what was taking place within. The front room on the first floor was fitted up with counters containing "dummy" drawers, and shelves ranged round the room were filled with empty cigar boxes. In the back room was a large empty wooden case. In the front top room I found about 120 square frames, made of quarter-inch deal boards, for which I could assign no use. In another room were a few framed oleographs, a portmanteau containing old clothes, shoes, etc., and a large quantity of shavings packed inside a counter. Everything seemed to point to preparations for a case of arson. I remarked to detective officers Standen and Manson, who were with me, "This place will most likely be heavily insured, and we shall evidently have to keep a sharp eye upon it." For some time I maintained a close watch upon the premises, occasionally meeting the young lady in charge, and she was very desirous of giving me all the information in her power, with a view to obtain whatever reward might be granted in the matter. On the Whit-Sunday I had a couple of detectives stationed in a room opposite the premises, so that they might notice what was going on, or follow anyone who left the place. At dusk they met me by appointment at a certain place, and reported that two men had entered the shop under very suspicious circumstances. One had gone up to the door, and after carefully looking round and seeing no one about had unlocked it. Whereupon the other, a gentleman-like person, quickly approached the door. They both darted inside, and the door was immediately closed. As both the men were still on the premises I took up a position where I had a full view of the door. About 9.50 p.m., the gentleman-like person came out and stood near a lamp in the road. I entered into conversation with two young ladies who were passing, and as we went by the individual referred to I recognised him as an old acquaintance, Mr O__, a solicitor.

This confirmed the statement of the lady assistant. For on questioning her as to how she procured the situation she had informed me that, having answered an advertisement, she was waited upon by the other partner, who informed her that Mr O__ had the making of the engagement, and that if she would be opposite the Post Office in Brown Street at half-past seven on a certain evening, she would meet with him. I now remembered - and the fact was a singular coincidence - that I had passed them at the very time mentioned at the appointed place, when Mr O__, noticing me, turned down a side street. After I had kept an eye on Mr O__ for some little time in Chorlton Road, the officers reported that the other man had locked the door, and was coming up the road. He immediately joined the solicitor, and they went down a number of side streets where they thought they would be likely to escape recognition. In Moss Lane they parted. One of them I knew. We therefore concentrated our attention upon the unknown person, whom we followed for a distance of two miles and a half and then saw him enter a house in Sussex Street, Broughton, with the number of which I was already familiar from a previous incident, which may be here briefly related.

One day a person in a highly excited state came to the Detective Office, bringing with him a circular which had been delivered at his address that morning. It ran as follows:-

"Sir, Knight, and Brother, - You are requested to attend the preceptory, No. 2,444 of St. John, Knight of Jerusalem, on __, 188_. Yours fraternally,

    "S__ K__."

I saw at once that it was a circular calling a meeting of some association; but the complainant protested that he did not belong to any such society, that he had no knowledge of "the

Knights of Jerusalem" or of "S__ K__," who addressed him so "fraternally."

Just at this time the newspapers teemed with the doings of the Fenian and American Dynamitards, and the foolish fellow had got it into his head that it was some "move" on the part of the "brotherhood," and that the penalty for non-attendance might be death. He went away, but came again in the evening in a cab, and was so terribly excited that I promised to make inquiries into the matter. Going to the address given, which was the very same house in Sussex Street, I found that so far from emanating from the "Fenian Brotherhood," the circular was a summons to attend a meeting of a lodge of their mortal enemies, the Orangemen, and that having been addressed to one of the members of the same name as the complainant, living in the same street, it had inadvertently been left at the wrong house. K__ at this time appeared to be a very respectable man.

Resuming the story of the Arson case, I remember that early the next morning I saw the landlord and agent of the property and ascertained the name of the person to whom the shop had been let. It appeared clear to me that both the men I had seen on the previous night were concerned with the matter. On Whit-Wednesday, the young lady assistant informed me that she had been paid a week's wages, and was told that as it was Whit-week she could have a holiday until the following Monday. On the Saturday I received information of a fire on the premises, and proceeding to the place found that the fire had been extinguished by the fire brigade. Mr. Superintendent Tozer and I examined the place, and I noticed that a number of the meerschaum pipes, cigar-holders, and oleographs were missing, and no trace of them could be found. On inspecting the gas-fittings, we found that they had been cut in several places in the shop, under the shop floor, in the cellar, under the stairs, under the boards in the front room of the first storey, and in the room over it. Two pipes had also been specially laid from the original work of the plumber, for the purpose of conveying gas into different parts of the building, and these had neither burners nor taps. In order to start this mechanism, a piece of string had been tied to the handle of the main in such a manner that a person pulling the string from outside could turn on the gas. Phosphorus had also been put down in the premises to help on the flames. All this was made clear in an analysis conducted by the police surgeon, Dr. Heslop. The wave of flames could be distinctly traced to each of the pipes which had begun to effect their purpose. Fortunately the string had only partially done its work, for on being pulled, instead of turning on the gas, it had jerked the key on to the floor, and it could not be found by one of the firemen, who, smelling gas on entering the premises, ran to the meter to turn it off. The next morning I found string and handle complete. I took steps to secure the two men whom I had observed leaving the premises; but as it was a very delicate matter, I thought it best to use a little discretion. I had pointed out Mr O__ as he was leaving his chambers to the two officers who were acting with me. Placing them inside the shop, I gave instructions that if either of the two men appeared he was to be detained.

On Saturday no one came near the place, but on the following day a man appeared about noon, with the statement that he had been ordered to tale possession of the premises by his employer, and he produced a note containing the order which he stated had been sent to him. He pretended that he knew nothing of the fire, and made inquiries as to the damage done. One of the detectives in charge of the shop brought this man to me. I questioned him as to how he came into possession of the note. First he said it had been delivered to him by post; but on my asking for the envelope, he admitted that it had been delivered by a messenger, who was a stranger to him. He gave me the name of his employer, who I found was the person I had followed to Sussex Street. I procured a cab and we drove to this address, to find that the person I wanted had gone out and was not expected back until late at night. We then drove to 10, Greenheys Lane, the residence of his servant, whom I had detained. This was a tobacconist and confectioner's shop. On arriving, I jumped out of the cab and walked through the shop into the sitting-room, where a man was resting on the sofa. In answer to my inquiries, he admitted that he was Mr. K___, a builder, and a relative of the man who had brought the note. I told him that if he was interested in the shop in Chorlton Road, he had better take possession of it, otherwise he would have to pay the expenses of the police who were in charge. I added that it looked very queer that no one had been near the place since the fire. He said that the shop did not belong to him; he had simply been doing some joinery work for Mr O___, the proprietor. I asked, "Where is Mr O___?" As he did not reply, I produced the letter, saying, "This is from him." He answered, "Yes, I met him this morning coming in from London, but he did not know that the place had been burnt down until I told him." I then said, "The best thing that you can do is to find Mr O___."

He was beginning to move for this purpose, when a woman who was present turned to him with the questions - "What have you to do with this?" "Where did you leave Mr O___?" He replied, "At his office, in Wellington Chambers." Having ascertained this, he, I, his servant, and a detective officer got into the cab and drove to the address mentioned.

K__ opened the front door with a latch-key, and we ascended the stairs to the third floor. K__ knocked at the door, and O__ opened it. We walked into an office or waiting-room, and O__ requested me to take a seat. He then walked into his private office, and I followed him. On the desk lay two books open. He immediately closed one, and was in the act of closing the other when I seized it across the table, and succeeded in placing my thumb between the pages where it had been open. It was Taylor's "Medical Jurisprudence," page 242, and treated on combustible materials. The particular page that he had been reading was on phosphorous. O__ sat down, when I said, "You know me, Mr O__, and I have come to see you about the fire in Chorlton Road." In answer to my inquiries he admitted that the shop belonged to him, and that it was insured in the Westminster Fire Office for £950. At first he said he did not know where the policy was, but on my threatening to search the premises he went to a deed-box and produced it. I then told them I should take them both into custody for conspiring together to set fire to the premises with intent to defraud. I was threatened with actions for libel, illegal arrest, and false imprisonment; was asked to show my warrant, and, after several other legal quibbles, O__ refused to go to the Detective Office unless I put my hands upon him, to enable him to take proceedings for an assault. He dared me to do so. K__ at the same time began to move towards the stairs, with the evident intention of getting away; but my colleague followed and seized him, whilst I secured Mr O__. Hauling him out of the office I closed the door behind me, forced him down stairs, and into the cab. The other man, who was simply a tool of the prisoners, we let go, informing him that we might require him, but would let him know. We drove to the Detective Office, where I informed them that I had been keeping observations on the shop for some time, and that I had seen them both leave the premises. As neither of them made any reply, the charge was entered. I asked O__ if he chose to account for himself on the Friday and Saturday? He replied that on the former day he was at Belle Vue Gardens, and on the following day at "Stockport and that road." He declined to answer any further questions. I asked K__ who had fixed the gas fittings, and he said he did not know, as O__ had engaged the man. On further questioning O__ by himself, he said that K__ had engaged him, but on confronting the prisoners O__ admitted that he engaged him. He declined to give any further information. The same day I searched O__'s apartment at 40, Cornbrook Grove, where I discovered the oleographs and other valuables which I had failed to find in the shop, as they had been removed before the fire. The next day I searched his office, and found a quantity of papers and books.

When the prisoners were brought before the Stipendiary Magistrate evidence was produced which showed that K__ had rented the shop in Chorlton Road, under the pretence of setting up his two daughters as milliners and dressmakers, and that the rent was paid regularly by him down to the date of the fire. From the papers which I discovered in the office, I produced a document purporting to transfer the premises from K__ to O__. Evidence was also given to show that K__ was constantly working at the shop, and that the policy of insurance was effected on the 8th of June. A short time before the fire the young lady assistant proved the amount of the takings, and also that she had orders to leave the shop before there was any necessity to light the gas. She also spoke as to the visits of the prisoners. The police fully substantiated the allegations made in the previous part of this story. Among the documents found I produced one which represented that £1 17s. 3d. was the total value of the stock in the shop.

On this evidence the prisoners were committed to the Assizes. The trial took place on the 20th July, 1886, before Mr. Justice Cave, when they were charged with wilfully and maliciously setting fire to a shop; also with conspiring together to set fire to the shop at 24, Chorlton Road. Mr. H. W. West, Q.C., the Recorder of Manchester, and Mr. Richard Smith appeared for the prosecution; and the prisoners were defended by Mr. J. Addison, Q.C., the Recorder of Preston, Mr. Cottingham, and Mr. Bradbury. Both prisoners were found guilty. O___ was sentenced to ten years' penal servitude, and K___ to seven years' penal servitude.

13

A SCENE IN COURT

I n the year of 1884 I was instructed to institute inquiries into a case of "robbery from the person with force." Whenever a report with such a heading comes into the hands of an experienced officer, he looks upon it as a most important matter, and always considers it a special duty to clear the books of this class of crime.

A Mr.___, from Edinburgh, was in Manchester on business when he was accosted by a man named Jack Savery, in the neighbourhood of the Globe Public House, in Gartside Street. The gentleman, who was a stranger to the town, was accosted by this worthy, who was a very old hand at the game, and after a few moments' conversation the son of Scotia found himself embracing mother earth. On getting over his surprise and gaining his feet, he found that he was minus his watch and chain and that his new acquaintance had suddenly disappeared.

The case was immediately reported to the police, and a very good description of Jack was given. It appeared that the complainant had told him he was leaving that night for the North; but the son of Scotia now said he would remain any length of time to have the offender brought to justice, for to be robbed of his watch and chain, as well as to receive a violent blow, was more than our Edinburgh friend could stand.

After receiving particulars of the case I went into the neighbourhood of Gartside Street, and very speedily heard that the "Terror" (Jack Savery) had been at work on the Saturday night. Soon afterwards I saw Jack coming along the street towards me, and knowing his dangerous character I was quite prepared for a tussle. Before reaching me, however, he turned into a shoe dealer's and leaned with his face and body over the counter. For a few minutes I was at a loss to know whether Jack was reaching a tool from the shoemaker's stool or was trying to hide his features from me. I, however, entered the shop, and addressing him said, "Well, Jack, I am looking for you. I want you to just go with me to the Town Hall." I took hold of him, and to my surprise he walked quickly along with me. At the Town Hall I placed him with seven others, and the prosecutor immediately identified him, at the same time remarking that he could pick him out of a thousand.

"Could you tell the other?" asked an Inspector who was standing by.

"No," replied the Scotchman.

I was rather surprised at the question as no mention had up to this been made of a second man, when the question was repeated and the same reply given. I then asked the prosecutor whether any other man had spoken to him or struck him, and he replied in the negative.

On the following morning Jack was committed to take his trial at the Sessions. When called upon for his defence, he proceeded to say that the prosecutor had failed to identify another who had been arrested for the robbery, and called upon the Inspector to substantiate his statement. The prosecutor and myself were recalled, and both denied the statement. The jury found the prisoner guilty, and he was sentenced to eight years' penal servitude.

An inquiry was afterwards instituted, when it was proved beyond all doubt that the Inspector, instead of attending to the solemn duty of an identification, was indulging in a practical joke. This led to the discovery of other irregularities, and the result was that the Inspector was asked to resign, and he retired on superannuation.

After Savery was sentenced, he sent the following letter to his father:

> "Her Majesty's Prison, Manchester,
> "12th February, 1884.

"Dear Father,

"Come up and see me as I have got eight years. I want to see you. I will tell you more when you come.

> "Your affectionate son,
> "J. SAVERY."

Shortly afterwards I received a visit from his father who wished to know if the reward was still available for the recovery of the watch, the son having heard the prosecutor say that he would give twenty shillings reward for its recovery and pay all expenses. I told him the reward still stood good in our books, and it then appeared that the son, anxious to get the reward for his father, had sent for him to the gaol and told him that the watch was pledged at a pawnbroker's in Chester Road for 8s., in the name of John Bates, of 20, Paradise Court. On learning this I went to the shop of

Mr. Tatton, pawnbroker, Chester Road, and recovered the property.

Jack has returned, and the first time he saw me after he came back, he called out, "I nearly done you, but the twelve (meaning the jury) would not have it. Didn't Inspector ___ fizz well? One of my companions got it up from hearing him talk in a public-house one night."

It appeared that the Inspector had been talking of the practical joke he had attempted to play upon the Scotch-man, when the idea seized a "pal" of Jack's to try to turn it to good account by calling upon the Inspector to prove that some other person than Jack had been arrested for the robbery whom the Scotchman had failed to identify, thus casting a doubt upon the identification.

14

MANCHESTER ANARCHISTS AT WORK

Towards the close of September, 1893, complaints were made by residents of obstruction, on Sunday mornings, at Ardwick Green, by a number of irresponsible young men who called themselves the "Manchester Anarchist Communist Group." It was very difficult to make out what these foolish fellows advocated, their principles appearing to be "What's yours is mine, and what's mine's my own." But it was also complained that very strong language was used, which tended to a breach of the peace. One of the speakers at the early meetings was the notorious Samuels, of whom it was stated in the House of Commons (see *Times*, September 22nd, 1893) that he gave the following counsel to the miners, who were then out on strike: "If they did not go in a body and fight, let them do it individually, with torch, knife, and bomb." Again, he is reported to have described the bomb outrage at the Barcelona Theatre as "a great and good act."

At length a deputation of the residents of the neighbourhood waited upon the Chief Constable, and asked that the police should interfere and put a stop to what had become a serious nuisance. The Chief Constable, after hearing the views of the deputation, attended these meetings and tried to reason with the obstructionists, pointing out to them that it was a very improper place to hold their meetings and offering them the use of Stevenson Square, where they could air their grievances from morning till night without being interfered with. It was only when matters grew worse, and a gentleman who expressed disapproval of the speakers' views had to be protected by the police, that the Chief Constable decided to interfere.

On Sunday, October 1st, I went to the green with Sergeant Dutton, in accordance with instructions, and found the Chief Constable present. About 11.30 a Belgian named Pellier, mounted a chair, and began to address a crowd of several hundred people, his remarks being of a revolutionary character. The drift of the argument of this "Solomon" appeared to be that if all the land was cultivated, and everybody did his fair share of labour ("Which tha won't" shouted one of the crowd), two hours a day would suffice. Under this new millennium there would be no unemployed, and no paupers ("And no spouters," chimed somebody).

He had been speaking for some time when the Chief Constable desired me to tell him that he would be glad to have a few words with him. Pellier at once got down from his chair, when the Chief Constable told him that the meeting was an obstruction and could not be allowed to go on; but no objection would be offered if they adjourned to Stevenson Square; or any of the Police Yards were open to them. Pellier replied that he had no wish to create a disturbance. He had a wife and family and had no desire to get into trouble, and would advise the meeting to break up. He then walked away. His place on the chair, however, was immediately taken by a young fellow named Alfred Barton, who was at once pulled down, when another man mounted the chair. When he in turn was seized, the rostrum was taken by a young mechanic named Patrick McCabe, who also fell into the hands of the police.

Things were now getting lively. The crowd had become excited. When McCabe was pulled off the chair, a shout was raised, and a general rush was made in the direction of the eight or nine policemen present. A young fellow named Barton seized the chair, which had served as a rostrum, and aimed a blow at me with it, hitting me on the chest, whilst some one struck me on the back of my head, knocking off my hat. To defend myself I grasped my umbrella and struck out right and left until I had cleared a space around me. In doing this I injured my umbrella, for which these young gentlemen had to pay, and it afterwards became a historical article in the annals of the Manchester Anarchist Group; for "Caminada and his gamp" (umbrella) was one of the texts upon which these juveniles founded their lectures. Burrows was not taken at the meeting, but was afterwards arrested in Fairfield Street, where he was heard to remark, "If I had a revolver I would blow the d__d policeman's brains out." After the arrests the meeting soon dwindled away.

On Monday morning, the precincts of the court were besieged by a large crowd of persons anxious to witness the trial of the defendants, and when the doors were thrown open to the public, both the sitting and standing accommodation was quickly taken up, the occupants of the gallery being chiefly friends of the prisoners.

The prisoners were Patrick McCabe, mechanic, aged 20,

William Haughton, pattern maker, aged 20, Ernest Stockton, engineer, aged 19, and Henry Burrows, clerk, aged 19. Such were the youths who had undertaken to introduce a new *régime* into the government of the country, and to convert the people of Manchester to views which they did not understand themselves.

Upon the case being called, McCabe became very excited, and began to exclaim that his friends were being kept out of the court by the police. This was denied, and, in response to Mr. Headlam, the prisoners called out the names of certain persons whom they wished to call as witnesses. These having been brought in and McCabe appeased, Haughton commenced to shout that they had been already tried and condemned by the press, which assertion drew from the Stipendiary Magistrate the remark that it was no good talking like that, as he ignored the press in such matters, and only went by the evidence given in court. The prisoner, however, continued to shout; but Mr. Headlam declined to hear him.

The evidence was continually interrupted by Burrows shouting "It's a lie," and by derisive laughter and hisses by the friends of the Anarchists in the gallery, which led the Stipendiary to threaten to have that portion of the court in which they were seated cleared. The prisoners cross-examined the witnesses in a very loud and insolent manner. Haughton began by remarking that "Caminada had a bad memory, like all policemen." Stockton commenced by informing the bench that he weighed 6 stone 5 pounds, to which I remarked that he "weighed a good deal more in cheek."

Before the whole of the evidence had been given, Mr. Headlam said he was satisfied. Whereupon the prisoners asked that the Chief Constable should be put into the witness-box. On this being complied with, Burrows asked him to "point out the brute who struck him," and the Chief Constable replied that he thought it was Caminada. He further stated that he had attended these meetings and warned the Anarchists of the consequences, and it was only when they grew worse, and it became a question as to whether the law or the Anarchists was to be master, that he had interfered. Burrows then put a number of irrelevant questions to Mr. Wood, which the latter could not answer, and as he left the witness-box Haughton shouted, "Are we to be gagged? He is in the hole and wants to get out of it." McCabe also commenced to shout, and for a few moments the court was a scene of uproar. Several witnesses were called on behalf of the Anarchists, all their own friends, to prove that there was no obstruction; but the Court was satisfied, and indicted a fine of 21 s. and costs, or in default, one month's imprisonment.

All, however, was not yet over, for immediately on hearing the decision one of the prisoners raised the cry "Hurrah for Anarchy," and this was taken up by Mr. Alfred Barton, another of these renovators of the world, aged 25, and following the occupation of a clerk, who, on leaving the court, shouted, "To h__l with law and order." This hater of the law was immediately arrested, and hauled before its representative. In answer to Mr. Headlam, this terrible fellow, who proposed to turn the world upside down, admitted that he had made use of the expression, but only did so because he was indignant at the way in which his comrades had been treated "for doing their duty;" the presumption, of course, being that their duty and obedience to the Anarchist group came before their duty as citizens, and ought therefore to be approved rather than punished. Mr. Headlam, however, refused to take this view of the case,

and Mr. Alfred Barton was bound over, in his own recogni-
sance of £5, to keep the peace for six months.
Notwithstanding his hatred to all "law and order," he
consented to be so bound, and the "tyrannical" fines of his
colleagues or "comrades," as they love to call each other,
were paid.

One of the principal Manchester papers, commenting
on the affair, said:-

"In Manchester there is a handful of persons who
delight in regarding themselves as Anarchists. They are
chiefly tailors, and some of them allow their hair to grow
long. There is nothing they dislike more than the laws and
regulations provided for the peace and safety of the popula-
tion. They cannot endure restraint. It is all very well for
common people to be compelled to conform to orders, but
they prefer to please themselves. There are few things they
are more desirous of doing than the things which the
authorities say must be left undone, and there is nothing
belonging to other people in which they do not claim to
have a proprietary interest. Their motto is, in effect, 'What's
yours is mine, and what's mine is my own.' They are always
amiable when they are permitted to defy the law and put
other people to loss and inconvenience. To restrain them
from doing these things is to offend them, and when they
are offended they are terrible people. They are invariably
fluent of speech, and their vocabulary is largely composed
of epithets of an irritating and alarming kind. In
Manchester the authorities have an objection to persons
obstructing the thoroughfares. They seem to fancy it is their
business to prevent the inhabitants from being inconve-
nienced by such proceedings. That is not the view the Anarchists take. It is all very well for ordinary citizens to be
bound down by such tyrannical restrictions, but Anarchists

are not ordinary beings. They chafe at law, and have no particular partiality for order. As a rule they have no worldly possessions, and they very much object to other people differing from them in that respect. They are in reality very peculiar people. But, as there are peculiar people who are law-abiding and inoffensive, they prefer to be known as Anarchists, which is supposed to mean something very different. There are open spaces in Manchester which may be used on a Sunday by people afflicted with crazes which they like to air in public. In such places such crazes may not be promulgated without offending anybody. They are not the places for Anarchists. What is the use of being Anarchists unless they can be offensive, and can interfere with the comfort and safety of other people? Holding a meeting in Stevenson Square, or on a police drill ground, on a Sunday, would not do any harm to anybody, therefore the Manchester members of this singular Order determine to hold their meetings on the high road. They held one on Sunday morning and created a serious obstruction. The police had the temerity to interfere. They actually stopped the meeting, and marched some of the more persistent of the ringleaders to the Police Office. That was more than Anarchical flesh and blood could stand, and they showered anathemas on their captors and their sympathisers, and solemnly warned them of bombs. With surprising indifference the police actually went the length, yesterday, of taking them before the magistrates, and Detective-Inspector Caminada had the audacity to speak of them as prisoners. They regarded the whole proceeding with lofty disdain, expostulated with the Stipendiary Magistrate on his want of due perspicacity, and denounced the prosecution as an attack upon freedom of speech. Whatever would they have said had they been members of the House of Commons during the 'discussion' of the Home Rule Bill? However, Mr. Headlam was callous of consequences. He seemed to be indifferent to the terrors consequent upon an offence against the Anarchists, and he actually imposed a substantial penalty upon them for inconveniencing their neighbours by obstructing the high road. What will happen now? Perhaps they will take possession of the Mayor's parlour, or the Chief Constable's private office for their next meeting. Such a proceeding would certainly inconvenience fewer persons than that for which they have been subjected to the indignity of arrest and punishment."

The gentleman referred to in a preceding paragraph, who allowed his hair to grow long, was of course the Anarchist poet; like the strength of Samson, the wisdom of the man did not lie in his head but in the hair outside it, and for that reason was afraid of having it cut, lest the poetical instinct should depart. On such a historical occasion as this, the first prosecution of the Anarchists in Manchester, the poet was called upon to take up his lyre and compose an ode to perpetuate the memory of the martyrs, and execrate their persecutors. What poet would not wish for such a theme? How the old Welsh harpist would have revelled in such a subject! Alas! how we are degenerated. It is enough to make Apollo weep! But our Anarchist laureate is not an ordinary being, and it would be well for some of our poets to look to their laurels. After lying on his back for some time, seeking for inspiration, he sang:-

THE SCAMP WHO BROKE HIS GAMP AT ARDWICK
GREEN, O.
Tune - MONTE CARLO

The Anarchists held meetings that were orderly and good,
And the workers they did go
Just to hear the Anarchists show
How the rich church-going thieves live upon their sweat
and blood,
And how the masters try and (*sic*) crush them low.

Chorus.
And as they walk about the street
With an independent air,
The people all declare,
They must have knowledge rare;
And they do say,
We wish the day,
When Anarchists shall have fair play,
And hold their meetings free at Ardwick Green, O.

But Nunn he was a bigot and he didn't like the truth,
And he to the meetings went,
On making mischief bent.
He got policemen and detectives to attack them without
ruth-
I think it's time that he to heaven was sent.

Chorus.
And as he walks about the church
With an hypocritical air,
The people all do swear,
He is a humbug rare,
For he does yell,
And the people tell,
That all (who) *think* will go to hell,
The parson who interfered at Ardwick Green, O.

Caminada showed his valour by knocking people down,
And using his gamp well,
Good citizens to fell.
He collared all the Anarchists, and marched them through
the town,
And put them in the Fairfield station cell.

Chorus.
And he walks along the street
With an independent air,
The people all declare,
He is a scoundrel rare,
His head is "Wood,"
And is no good,
Except to provide the pigs with food,
The scamp who broke his gamp at Ardwick Green, O.

He brought them before the beak, and thought to give it
them hot,
But his little game was off,
And he got it rather rough,
The Anarchists did bravely, and of cheek give him a lot,
And it won't be very long before he's had enough.

Chorus.
And as he walks along the court
With a "big bug" sort of air,
The people all declare,
Oh! what a fall was there.
And they are sure,
He will never more
The Anarchists attempt to floor,

The D. who broke his gamp at Ardwick Green, O.

He told a lot of thumpers, and spun some awful fibs,
But they soon proved him to be
A liar of high degree.
And though Headlam, like an idiot, made them fork out
their "dibs,"
They fairly got old Cam. up a tree.

Chorus.
And he walks about the street,
With an independent air,
The people all do swear,
He is a detective rare,
For he can lie,
And none can vie-
In the list of scamps, none stands so high
As the D. who broke his gamp at Ardwick Green, O.

But the time is coming quickly when Cam. will repent
Of having tried his game
The Anarchists to lame,
Or he and his d__d crew will to that warm land be sent,
And never trouble honest folks again.

Chorus.
And he walks along the court,
With a hanging vicious air,
The people will declare,
Oh! what an awful scare.
And they will cry,
Oh! let him die,
And deep down the gutter lie

The D. who broke his gamp at Ardwick Green, O.

IT IS SAID that there is only one stop between the sublime and the ridiculous. The sublimity of the profession of a poet is no doubt something grand. But the productions of some of these versifiers are the merest rubbish, and our readers must excuse me for inflicting upon them a copy of the Anarchist laureate's effusion, our object being to show the grand and noble ideas held by these martyrs to the cause of disorder. The idea of sending the reverend gentleman to heaven, and the detectives to a "warmer land," where of course there are no "honest folks," is very suggestive. But I suppose we must content ourselves by knowing we are placed in the same category as lawyers, whom we know, according to the old adage, have a very great difficulty entering into the kingdom of heaven. As regards their being "sure" that "he (Caminada) will never more the Anarchists attempt to floor," the writer has come to the conclusion that it is never safe to prophesy unless you know.

Having encouraged themselves by the strains of poetry, and got up their courage to the sticking point, they vowed vengeance on the immortal "gamp" and its owner. The next thing was to get a number of handbills printed, calling a meeting, which would be held at Ardwick Green, on the following Sunday morning, "in spite of Caminada and his crew," to defend the right of freedom of speech. These were distributed throughout the city; whilst some of these terrible gentlemen, armed with paste-can and brush, occupied themselves at midnight in pasting the walls of St Thomas's churchyard - of which church the Rev. Canon Nunn is the rector - with these handbills, taking care, however, to place sentries to give the alarm in case of the approach of a policeman.

Sunday arrived, and there was a crowd of several hundred people at the meeting-place, most of whom had turned up, as they expressed it, "to see the fun." About 11.30 a young fellow, named Patrick John Kelly, about 22 years of age, and who followed the business of a taxidermist, mounted the rostrum, and the crowd gathered round. He commenced - "Comrades and working-men, I come here on behalf of my comrades who were locked up last Sunday morning. In spite of Caminada and the police we are going to hold our meeting." He got no further, for he was immediately pulled off the chair, on which he cried, "Three cheers for Anarchy and revolution;" but his invitation met with no response. As he was rushed down to Fairfield Street Police Station a large crowd followed, mostly out of curiosity to get a glimpse him. To these he kept appealing, "If you are men be men," evidently inviting a rescue, but the crowd only laughed at him.

When brought before Mr. Headlam, at the Police Court, in reply to the magistrate he said that he was charged under a law that was passed by a section of society calling themselves Government, and passed by them regardless of the interests of other people. He was charged with an obstruction of the public highway, although how it could be a public highway when the public were not allowed to use it he failed to see. He was quite aware that the Anarchists had been told that they could go to Stevenson Square and hold their meetings. But what was the good of that? The people would not come to them, so they had to go to the people. He compared Caminada's making his comrades pay for the umbrella, which he broke over their heads in the mêlée, to the Government charging the Featherstone miners for the bullets with which they were shot. The meetings would go on, and men would be found week by week to speak, and ready to go to prison if necessary in defence of their rights. Mr. Headlam cut the harangue short with "21s. and costs, or in default one month!" and the martyr, Joseph Patrick Kelly, who failed to see the difference between using and obstructing a public highway, was hurried below until the fine was paid, as he was not quite "ready to go to prison in defence of their rights."

Handbills were again put out setting the authorities at defiance and announcing that the Anarchists were determined to hold their meeting on Sunday morning next, October 16th. The contest between the upholders of law and order and those of Anarchy and disorder had now become the talk of the town. The consequence was that a crowd of 3,000 or 4,000 persons was drawn together from mere curiosity, necessitating a large staff of police. The people were kept on the move, and as the Anarchists appeared they were ordered away. At length a young fellow, named James Coates, a lithographic printer, seized the opportunity to mount the rostrum, and said he was there to protest against the action of Canon Nunn, in interfering with the right of free speech, aided by "a man called Caminada." He was taken into custody, and a number of his comrades who pressed round were also arrested and taken to Fairfield Street Police Station. Here two men, named Taylor and Payne, who had taken part in the obstruction at Ardwick Green, and had followed the prisoners down, applied to give bail for two of their comrades, but as they did not know the names of the men for whom they offered bail, they were told to go to the Town Hall. This they refused to do or to leave the office, and had to be ejected. They were subsequently arrested for causing an obstruction in Fairfield Street.

Next morning (Monday) the following prisoners were brought before the magistrates: Arthur Booth, joiner, aged

32; Max Falk, tailor, aged 28; Abraham Lewis, tailor, aged 21; James Coates, lithographic printer, aged 21; Edmund George Taylor, tutor, aged 51; Thomas Spaine, shoemaker, aged 26; Walter Payne, clerk, aged 29; William Downey Allen, printer, aged 26; James Beale, porter, aged 28; Charles Watts, newsagent, aged 23; and William Lancaster, labourer, aged 28.

In reply to the bench the prisoners denied that there was any obstruction. Coates, who read his reply, which had evidently been prepared for him, created much amusement. He said the character of the prosecution was utterly absurd, and "initiated by parsons." They expected no justice in the law courts, which were only places of villainy and hypocrisy. The whole had been done at the bidding of that "sanctimonious parasite, Nunn." Spaine, Beale, and Lancaster were fined 21s. and costs, or in default one month's imprisonment; the rest were fined 40s. and costs, or a month's imprisonment.

On the following Sunday the police were present in considerable force in view of a possible demonstration. Some thousands of people turned up, apparently out of curiosity, and rushed backwards and forwards through the neighbourhood in rather an alarming manner, as reports were raised as to the presence of some of the martyrs. The crowds, however, were kept under control until the public-houses opened, when, without enjoying any further excitement, they dispersed. These meetings were a little harvest for the publicans of the neighbourhood, some of whom had to engage extra waiters for Sundays during the agitation.

It afterwards appeared that the reason for the absence of the apostles of disorder was a compact made with Dr. Sinclair the night previous; the Anarchists promising to hold no meeting until he put their case before the authorities. Accordingly on October 25th Dr. Sinclair brought the matter before the City Council. He pointed out that the offenders were a lot of foolish young men, and suggested that the press should let all decent citizens understand that the Lord Mayor personally would be glad if they would stay away from Ardwick Green, and leave those young men severely alone. If some means could be taken to bring the meetings into ridicule there would be a chance of finding a remedy. He also expressed an opinion that the police had acted in a very high-handed, hasty fashion, which was met with cries of "No."

Mr. Rawson replied that it was only because there was a danger of disturbance in the public thoroughfares that action by the police had been taken. There was no ground whatever for the insinuation that the Watch Committee was actuated by any desire to suppress free speech. The whole question was one of ruling the town. The police did not interfere until all means of private persuasion had been tried and failed. Mr. Alderman Lloyd added that, in addition to seriously obstructing the traffic, the language used by these men was at times of a disgusting nature. Mr. Alderman Mark, chairman of the Watch Committee, handed round a collecting box, amidst much amusement, on which the words "Manchester Anarchist Group" were embroidered in black satin. It did not come to my knowledge whether any of the worthy councillors subscribed, or what the alderman would have done with the money had they done so.

As the Anarchists - who, though they object to the laws, do not hesitate to appeal to the authorities when it suits them - did not attain their object, the following handbill was issued:-

"The Anarchists and Ardwick Green! Obstruction or

Oppression? The City Council uphold Perjury and Violence! Overtures of Peace rejected! Caminada authorised to break the heads of Manchester Citizens! This Tyranny shall not succeed! The Anarchists will be at Ardwick Green on Sunday next, October 29, at 11-30. An Indignation Meeting will be held in Stevenson Square at 3. Attend in your thousands!"

The consequence was that a great crowd congregated on the Sunday morning, which was kept running in different directions as various false rumours of arrests or other excitement cropped up. For wherever there is anything to be seen an Englishman must go and see it; and in the eager warmth of excited spirits he will run after it. No matter whether caravan or carriage; no matter whence it comes or whither it goes; no matter whether its contents be a kangaroo or a cannibal chief, a giraffe or a princess, Rusty Fusty, a baboon, or an Anarchist, the interesting stranger is cheered with enthusiasm, and speeds along graced with all the honours of extemporaneous popularity.

At length, as the crowd, weary of waiting, was beginning to disperse, Herbert Stockton, a bookmaker, about 23 years of age, and a relative of one of the previous martyrs, was seen crossing the park accompanied by about 200 people, and, taking his stand upon the pedestal of the lamp in the centre of the five cross roads, commenced to address the crowd, but was at once removed. It was my intention to have let him go and to issue a summons against him; but he said that he did not want any quarter from the police or from the authorities. His friends would persist in holding the meetings, and the police had better give it up as a bad job.

In reply to the magistrates Stockton said that it seemed to him that by adopting a police censorship policemen were to have the power of telling the citizens of Manchester what they should listen to, and what they should not. That might of course do for Russia, but it was not the right sort of thing for Manchester. In their own case they were fighting for freedom of speech - for which their ancestors died - and they were not going to let that right be taken from them without a struggle. They were not going to be ridden over roughshod by the police, the parsons, or anyone else. Mr. Armitage pointed out from the bench that it was not a question of liberty of speech; for there were at least half a dozen places in the city where the defendant and his friends could express their opinions from morning till night if they liked; but they were determined that "they would be a law unto themselves." He would be fined 40s. and costs, or one month's imprisonment, and if he came again he would be sent to gaol without the option of a fine. The fine was paid.

The struggle still went on. The public were informed, by means of handbills, that on the following Sunday "the sermon would be preached by an Anarchist, the lessons read by Chief Inspector Caminada, and the psalms sung by his crew" (detectives), the people being asked to assemble in their thousands. They did so. The crowd reached from the lamp opposite Brunswick Street to Rusholme Road in one direction, and extended up Brunswick Street, Hyde Road, Stockport Road, and Higher Ardwick, in other directions, the park and its environs being crowded.

At the appointed time, the candidate for martyrdom, James Birch, a mechanic, about 21 years of age, mounted the lamp, and, striking a dramatic attitude, waved a baton in the shape of a rolled up newspaper to attract attention. His speech, the delivery of which was stopped rather abruptly, was accompanied by a blaze of fireworks. It was the Fifth of November, and a number of youths thought it a good opportunity of keeping up the holiday. The would-be martyr was soon the target for the squibs, crackers, and other fireworks, and the cry was raised, "Duck him in the horse trough," which stood near for the purpose of watering horses. He was then taken into custody, so much of his speech as he could deliver being of the usual character: "He himself would fight the matter to the bitter end, and it was intended by himself and friends to hold meetings in spite of Canon Nunn and Caminada."

In Court he created great amusement by trying to read an evidently prepared defence. He described the prosecution as a "vexatious" one, got up by bigotted meddlers who wanted to interfere with the liberty of the citizens. The law, he said, was "sprained" in order to crush out the right of public meeting, and the charge of obstruction was "merely a fake." He denied being an Anarchist, but gloried in being a member of the Labour Church. All bodies, he continued, who worked on behalf of labour were with them in the struggle, and they would not be stamped out until the whole labour movement had been extinguished. A fine of 40s. and costs was imposed, which was again paid.

On the following Wednesday the terrible bomb outrage was committed at the Liceu Theatre, Barcelona, spreading death and destruction on all sides; and Europe stood aghast. Samuels, one of the earliest speakers at these Ardwick Green meetings, and connected we believe with an Anarchist periodical, described the deed as "a great and good act." Herbert Stockton, one of the Ardwick Green martyrs, whilst everyone was deploring the calamity, wrote to the *Manchester Guardian* (Nov. 11), and, after sounding the trumpet of the local Anarchists, said the Watch Committee were watching the effect of this suppression on the citizens, with a view to stopping all outdoor meetings of a political nature if possible. The Watch Committee had been badly beaten, and it was only a question of time as to when they would realise it.

On Sunday, the 12th of November, some thousands of persons again congregated at Ardwick Green, and the efforts of the police were chiefly directed to keeping them in motion and so preventing obstruction. Herbert Stockton at length mounted the lamp, and said they were determined to hold meetings in spite of Canon Nunn or anyone else. Whilst his "comrades" were shouting approval, a man quietly approached and, suddenly shoving his head between the speaker's legs, mounted him upon his back, and rushed off with him towards the water-trough, followed by an excited and approving crowd, who shouted, "Baptise him! Baptise him!" while the small knot of Anarchists looked on with dismay. The police promptly interfered, and rescued the youthful martyr from his tormentors; whilst he and several others were encouraging him to defy the law were arrested. On the way to the Police Station, a conversation took place in the cab between Birch and Stockton, with respect to bombs, which was overheard by a police officer, Stockton openly saying that their society was determined to hold their meetings at Ardwick Green, and that they should resort to extreme measures. The movement, he remarked, was going on all right, and they had got two or three Rothschilds behind them.

In response to the bench, Stockton said that the citizens of Manchester should be congratulated on having such a versatile detective inspector. He combined his ability as a detective with that of a stage manager. He managed a most beautiful and dramatic scene in which he (Stockton) was to be dipped in a water-trough. Mr. Headlam reminded the prisoner that he would have to prove such a statement, as it was denied; to which he replied, amidst some laughter,

"Well, I don't think I shall attempt to prove it." The reference to the bombs and Rothschilds, he said, was only a joke, and concluded by saying that the society had decided not to pay any more fines. Whatever punishment was inflicted on their members would, he supposed, have to be expiated in gaol. The same thing would happen to a dozen, to hundreds - he might say to thousands - of young men, who knew that the liberties of the people were in danger, and who were determined to do what they could to keep them safe. He, himself, if he was not in prison, was determined to address other meetings at Ardwick Green. Birch said that there were a great many determined to fight out the matter to the bitter end, no matter what treatment they received from the hands of the authorities, under laws passed by those classes of society who lived in luxury by the exploitation of labour.

If every person were to be allowed to repudiate the laws because they were passed by "classes" with whom they had no sympathy, I am afraid we should soon have a state of Anarchy which would bring even the Anarchists to their senses. These gentlemen work on an ideal state of society. They take every man and woman to be perfect; they make no allowance for different tastes, feelings, or inherited tendencies; nor have they any idea that the stronger would oppress the weak. Under their millennium every man would drop into his proper place; every woman would be mated with the right man; there would be no envy, hatred, uncharitableness, or laziness. Two hours a day's work, as one speaker said, would serve everybody, and the eight-hours-day would be knocked into a "cocked hat." Then I suppose we should be able to sing:-

Two hours work,
Twelve hours play,

Ten hours sleep,
For one "quid" a day.

BUT IN THESE good days there will be no use for money.
Every man will have what he wants, and there will be
rushing to obtain the best places. The anti-smoker will be
content to work to provide another man with tobacco; the
teetotaller will delight, by the sweat of his brow, to provide
the boozer with his beer; there will be no rows about
denominational education, for every religion will be
supported out of a common fund, and Secularists will not
grumble about it; adultery and theft will not be known;
government and law will not be needed; and lawyers,
judges, and policemen will be out of work. Oh, happy times!
Knowing, however, what we do about human nature, we are
afraid these youthful Anarchists will have a difficult job
before them before all this is brought about.

Herbert Stockton and James Birch, two old offenders,
were fined 30s. and costs, or in default one month's imprisonment, and to be bound over in two sureties of £25 for six
months; James Welling, a labourer, aged 24, 40s. and costs,
or one month; George Storey, a tailor, aged 49, 21s. and costs,
or one month; Alfred Roberts, dyer, aged 20, Robert
Warburton, warehouseman, aged 19, Frederick Froggat,
turner, aged 14, and James Taylor, warehouseman, aged 16,
were all bound over to one surety of £10 to keep the peace
for six months.

A local newspaper commented on these prosecutions in
the following terms:-

"The Manchester 'Anarchist group' still keep up their
Sunday recreation at Ardwick Green, and their Monday

privilege of being fined. The law has given them the notoriety they desired. Their wildest flights of fancy, their most
sweeping condemnations, would not have attracted more
than a handful of idlers had the law 'winked' at their
proceedings. Now, however, the obstruction has become
serious, and week after week the police 'vindicate the
majesty of the law' by arresting the bolder 'Anarchists.' But
that is all. The obstruction continues, and the people flock
to the Green in the hope of seeing some lively struggles
between the police and the Anarchists. Who will get tired of
this unseemly farce first, the police, the public, or the Anarchists? Perhaps, if a few of the people who assemble were
summoned with the Anarchists there would be less obstruction; but we doubt whether this would mend matters. On
the other hand, the law must be supreme. There are many
other places at which the Anarchists can meet; but, simply
because the police and public wish them to go elsewhere,
the 'group' invite the law to do its worst. It is all very silly
and foolish. The Anarchists are undoubtedly to blame,
because they have taken up a very idiotic attitude. Were any
religious body to cause a similar obstruction we should
strongly condemn it; and nothing can be further from the
truth than to say that the Anarchists are prosecuted because
they hold opinions with which we cannot agree. Dr. Sinclair
declares that the disturbances are largely owing to the
bureaucratic methods of the police authorities, and to the
violence employed by some officers. Whether this be true or
not, there is no excuse for the young men who wilfully
break the law. If no other site could be found the Anarchists
might receive some sympathy, but they gather together in a
forbidden place merely to defy the police and to show their
contempt for the law."

On the two following Sundays much the same thing

occurred, Henry Salop, a labourer, aged 26, being fined 40s. and costs, or a month, for the first meeting; and for the second, James Coates, who had previously been fined 40s. and costs, was ordered to find two sureties in £30 for six months, or in default one month's imprisonment.

By this time the public seemed to be losing interest in the struggle, and the meetings had dwindled to a few hundreds. The morning of Sunday, the third of December, was damp and raw, yet for nearly an hour the space encircling the lamp-post, which the Anarchists claimed as their forum, was patrolled by groups of people, looking suspiciously one upon another, and evidently impatient for someone to begin. Just as the crowd had reached its biggest dimensions, and was beginning to dwindle, Henry Burrows, one of the original offenders, advanced rapidly towards the lamp-post, where he was at once encircled by the people pressing in from every side. He began in a low, tremulous voice to address the meeting. I advised him to be quiet and go away, but he replied that nothing would prevent him and his friends from holding meetings there every Sunday. I asked him again to desist, but he continued speaking, the purport of his observations being that there would be another meeting there on the Sunday following, and one in Stevenson Square that afternoon. As he would not desist, a cab was hailed, in which he was placed, and driven away amidst general laughter.

In the court he described me as the biggest liar he had ever known, and on leaving the dock he called out, "Long live Anarchy!" He was bound over in two sureties of £30, or two months' imprisonment. Both he and Coates elected to go to prison, probably from the difficulty of finding bail. As the fines ceased to be paid, one or two of the other Anarchists had to go to gaol. At their meetings in Stevenson

Square, which were not interfered with, the collecting box was sent round every Sunday afternoon; but after the Barcelona outrage, followed by others, the subscriptions evidently dropped off. Then came the martyrdom. How they suffered it the following letters will show:-

"Strangeways,
"December 2, 1893.

"My dear Father,

"I am writing this in the depths of despair, to know if you will be one of the sureties of £30, and get Alf. or our Albert to be the other, and I will be bound myself in £50. I shall be eternally obliged if you would, for another week in here will drive me mad, I believe. Hoping you are quite well, and mother also,

"I remain,
"Your almost heart-broken son,

"JAMES COATES.

"P.S. - There are also 9s. in costs to pay, which please beg or borrow for me. I will pay it back if I have to starve. - JIM.

"P.S. - If you can't, please go to Bednal's and ask the boss. I think he will (Peter I mean). - JIM."

This letter was written six days after his conviction.

On the 27th of December Burrows wrote:-

"MY DEAREST FATHER,

"I am sorry to have to write this, but I am afraid my

health is giving way. Will you go to comrade Barton and ask him to send sureties AS SOON AS HE POSSIBLY CAN. I can't stand much more of this.

"With love to all,
"Your affectionate son,
"H. BURROWS.

"Barton's address is 13, Shaftesbury Street, C-on-M. - H.B."

ECCE HOMO - BEHOLD THE MAN! *Quantum mutatus ab illo* - How changed from what he once was!

Under the heading of "A 'Broken-hearted' Hero," a leading Manchester newspaper, commenting on the first letter, says :-

"By their weekly conflicts with the city police, the Manchester group of Anarchists have been trying to pose as heroes during the last few months; but it seems their courage and fortitude are by no means equal to their grandiloquence. One of the most valiant of the group was James Coates, who delighted his friends a week ago last Monday by telling Mr. Headlam, the stipendiary, before whom he appeared, that the sentences he imposed on his Anarchist comrades the week before were brutal, and that his remarks on that occasion were the most ridiculous nonsense man ever talked. Criticism so frank disturbed the stipendiary's official gravity, and he was constrained to join in the general laughter which it evoked. Coates, it will be remembered, defied the police on the previous Sunday by addressing an Anarchist meeting on forbidden ground at Ardwick Green. He declared that he should hold a meeting on the public highway, and assert the right of free speech in spite of both the law and the police. Yea, he was prepared to go to prison and to suffer death before he would forfeit that right. This speech could have been, in its way, a masterpiece of invective had it not been suddenly interrupted by Chief Inspector Caminada arresting him, for on his MSS. notes appeared, among other choice headings: 'Right of free speech in spite of bigot Nunn and his followers' - 'Cami. (Caminada) and his gamp' (the damaged umbrella the Anarchists had to pay for) - 'Caminada's crew' - 'Not to be daunted by Headlam's brutal sentences.' Coates, who had already been fined for a similar offence, was ordered to find two sureties of £30 each, and to be bound himself in £50 to be of good behaviour for six months. The one month's imprisonment in default, and the letter which was addressed by him to his father, show to the full extent of his valour and fine professions."

After quoting the letter the article concludes -

"Coates' friends are in no way disposed to remove him from his temporary confinement, and there is every probability that he will have to do his time."

In the meantime Messrs. E. G. Taylor and W. Payne had been complaining that they had not been justly dealt with, and after a newspaper correspondence, signing declarations, and failing to obtain what they considered satisfaction from the Watch Committee, on the 29th of November a public meeting was held in the Co-operative Hall, Downing Street, for the purpose of protesting against the violence and perjury of the police in connection with the arrest of the two gentlemen.

The meeting was not unanimous, and on occasions there were somewhat noisy manifestations of feeling. Mr. S. Norbury Williams, who had recently been elected Citizens'

Auditor, presided. He opened the meeting with a rather lengthy speech, but, instead of keeping to the subject for which the meeting was called, he wandered off to the particular topics which interested him as Citizens' Auditor, and amid cries of "That's old," "We've heard it all before," he began to inform the meeting how the councillors spent their money in wines, beer, mineral water, gloves, trips to Thirlmere, etc. Amid cries of "Keep to the subject," a lighted cracker was thrown into the middle of the hall, which created much confusion and alarm, many of the audience, having the bomb outrages on the Continent in mind, hastily decamping. Several others spoke, but crackers and fireworks continued to go off, causing confusion, and having a tendency to thin the audience. The chairman said that he believed a number of plain clothes men were in the room, and asked the audience to take down their names; but the audience did not appear to concern themselves about the matter. Two gentlemen then addressed the meeting, moving an amendment thanking the Watch Committee for the action they had taken in regard to the Anarchists; but the disorder became so great that the chairman appealed in vain for order, and described the proceedings as un-English. At length amid much noise a resolution was passed asking for an inquiry into the matter, and a deputation was appointed to present it. Then the meeting broke up, the audience on their way out running the gauntlet of a number of men with collecting boxes, seeking for coppers to defray the expenses.

In connection with the Downing Street meeting a question was asked in the House of Commons respecting the remarks of Mr. Charles Rowley, a Justice of the Peace, who took a prominent part in it, and he was called upon for an explanation.

As the Lord Mayor refused to receive the deputation, the matter was brought up in the City Council, by Dr. Sinclair, who expressed regret that the Watch Committee did not see their way to make inquiry; but the Lord Mayor ruled the matter out of order, and pointed out that it was a question for the law courts to settle. If any one had any complaint to make respecting the conduct of the police they might place a notice upon the agenda. No one, however, took the trouble to do this, and nothing further was heard of the matter, except the braggadocio of a few agitators who, as usual, said the matter could not rest where it was, and threatened all sorts of pains and penalties. But even these appeared to find out that the game was not worth the candle, and quietly collapsed.

The ridicule heaped upon the Anarchists on showing the "white feather," after their fine professions, made them a laughing stock, and things began to look very flat on Sunday mornings, and the crowds to diminish. No one, I presume, regretted the matter, except the publicans in the neighbourhood of the meeting place. On Sunday, the 10th of December, a change of tactics was tried. Patrick Joseph Kelly was seen approaching the Green, carrying his platform with him in the shape of a soap-box covered with white paper. He did not, however, make for the lamp, but on reaching the corner of Union Street, he placed his box on the ground, and mounting it proceeded to address the crowd. I asked him to move on, but he declined, and was taken into custody. His defence was that he was not guilty of obstruction as there was no one on the footpath at the time. He was fined 40s. and costs, or one month's imprisonment.

On the Sunday following, the martyr was William Haughton, who was bound in two sureties to keep the peace for six months, or one month's imprisonment.

On Sunday, the 24th, no martyr appeared, as probably none of them were inclined to eat their Christmas dinner in the police station. But on the 31st Morris Mendelssohn, a mackintosh maker, aged 24, made his first appearance, and commenced the New Year by being ordered to find two sureties of £10 each to keep the peace for three months, or to go to prison for a month; and then, as the public interest in the matter appeared to have died out, and the stock of "patriots and martyrs" seemed to have been exhausted, Ardwick Green assumed its normal condition. After a contest of three months the police were allowed to enjoy their Sundays in peace.

The generality of the speeches delivered by these men were of one type. After abusing Her Majesty and the Royal Family, and giving a version of their own respecting the emoluments of the Royal Family, they would go on to describe how many paupers might be kept in comfort if this money were divided amongst them. They would then turn their attention to the House of Lords, or, as they described it, the House of robbers and plunderers, and talk of the land stolen by their forefathers. "Every man," said one of these reformers, "should work two hours a day - no more and no less. All priests, parsons, bishops, and ecclesiastics of all sorts were useless and should be unfrocked. Policemen should be made to go down coal pits, and might thank their stars that they were not sent to even a deeper and hotter region. He would pay the national debt with a stroke of the pen. He would___" The sentence was incomplete, for a "stroke" on the side of the head brought him from his perch, and when taken to the Police Station and searched three-pence halfpenny in money and a collecting box, on which was written the "Manchester Anarchist Communist Group," was found in his possession.

The following handbill has recently been circulated in the neighbourhood of Gorton:-

"Commune of Paris!! The Manchester Anarchists will celebrate the Revolt of the Paris Workers against Master and Governments on Sunday, March 17th, 1895, in Stevenson Square, at 3 p.m.; New Cross (Oldham Road), at 8 p.m. Rebellion is Progress."

15

LONG FIRM FRAUDS

Long firm frauds are principally carried on by experienced swindlers, who work into each others' hands, and whilst at times very difficult to track they cause great loss to the mercantile community.

The first thing they do on commencing operations is to take an office or warehouse in some business part of the town, and to give orders for elaborately fitting and furnishing the same. They next proceed to the printer and stationer, to whom orders are given for business cards, invoices, books, circulars, etc. Having obtained these, the "firm" are now ready to commence business, and orders are given right and left for every conceivable article. If references are required these are offered to firms of "equal standing" with themselves, or in some cases no such name is to be found at the address given, and the postal authorities having received instructions to forward such letters to the address of the "long firm," these gentlemen then obtain the privilege of answering their own references.

The goods are always disposed of as fast as they can be

obtained, and when the day for payment arrives neither the members of the firm nor their references are to be found.

Some years ago, a warehouse was taken in Aytoun Street, Manchester, by a person who described himself as a "General Merchant." Having as usual fitted up the place elaborately, and furnished the offices in sumptuous manner - for which extravagance however, he never paid a penny - he and another of the "firm" commenced issuing orders for stationary, satteens, jeans, calicos, prints, silks, carpets, umbrellas, and any other kind of goods which they could by any means dispose of.

Their mode of procedure was first to request samples and prices of goods, which of course were promptly sent and quoted. After the lapse of a few days, so as not to give rise to suspicion by undue haste, the "firm" would despatch orders. In some cases where the amount was small, cash was paid. Thus confidence was created, and larger orders followed. At other times references were required, and these they had always ready, to vouch for their respectability, uprightness, integrity, and so on. In this way the swindlers managed in a short time to secure some thousands of pounds' worth of goods, which were immediately either pawned, sold by auction, or otherwise cleared. After a very brief career, the crash came, and on pay-day arriving both the principals of the "firm" and their "references" had disappeared.

A meeting was called of the victims of the conspiracy, and this was attended by several solicitors in the interests of their clients. I also was requested to be present. Some were for issuing writs; others for taking criminal proceedings. Ultimately it was agreed that they should consult an eminent criminal solicitor on the matter.

The carpet firm, however, believed that I had a good

criminal case, and determined to back me up. I therefore applied for warrants, which were granted, and I proceeded to the house of one of the partners, but was unsuccessful in finding any trace of him. I learned that a great quantity of goods had been removed from the warehouse by porters plying for hire. By means of these men and others, who were well paid for their time and trouble, I succeeded in tracing the goods to different places. At an auctioneer's I discovered a considerable portion of the missing goods, and in the office was shown a receipt for £100 in money as well as other memoranda relating to the exchange of goods for £250 worth of jewellery.

No trace of either of the partners could be traced for some time. At length a salesman, who knew one of them, on passing along Booth Street, recognised him in a cab, on top of which was a box similar to the one described by the woman of the house in which his partner lived as having been taken away with him. After some inquiries at the railway station I found a porter who had lifted such a box from a cab, and the time corresponded with the warehouseman's story, but the railway official could give me no further information. The next day I started for Liverpool, in search of the box, taking with me one of the salesmen from the carpet warehouse for the purpose of identifying its owner. As we were passing along the side of one of the docks in an omnibus, my companion suddenly exclaimed, "There's one of them!" Looking in the direction of his finger, I saw that he was pointing towards a gentleman who was carrying a black bag in one hand, and escorting a lady on his other arm. I jumped out of the 'bus, and, hurrying after him, took him to the station, where, on searching the bag, I found in it the jewellery which had been exchanged for the goods. I also discovered amongst his property a card of his partner's, bearing the address ___, Islington, London.

After bringing the prisoner to Manchester, I saw the principal of the firm of carpet manufacturers, who gave me £20 to go to London and continue my search for the other partner. After a couple of days' inquiry, I went to the address indicated upon the card, carrying a large paper parcel, and asked for Mr. D___.

I was told that he had not yet come down stairs. Intimating that my business was important, and that I would speak to him at his bedroom door, I walked upstairs before anyone could interfere with me, and, entering the bedroom, saw from the description given to me that I had run my man to earth.

"Are you Mr. D__?" I asked.

"Yes."

"Have you seen Mr. C__ in London?"

"No; I don't know where he is; we have dissolved partnership. What is it you want?" he inquired, somewhat anxiously.

Looking round, I saw a portion of the property that had been described to me in Manchester, and then said:

"I have a warrant for your arrest."

Jumping up suddenly he seized a razor, with the evident intention of committing suicide. I flew at him. A struggle ensued for the possession of the dangerous instrument, and I was successful in wresting it from him; but so violent was he that I was compelled to handcuff him. Having brought him to Manchester, he and his confederate were committed to the Assizes, where they were tried before Mr. Justice Brett, at the January Assizes, 1880, on seven counts, for conspiring together and fraudulently obtaining goods from various persons.

Having been found guilty, a previous conviction for fraud was proved against C__ for which he was sentenced to nine months' imprisonment at Clerkenwell Sessions, 1873. He was now sentenced to seven years' penal servitude, and D__ to five years' penal servitude.

16

THE ARREST OF MR. WILLIAM O'BRIEN, M.P., IN MANCHESTER

T he last decade in the history of the empire has been full of stirring political incidents. It is within the recollection of all what a sensation was caused when a world-renowned statesman suddenly sprung a Home Rule scheme upon his party and the country, and since then a constant series of startling events have followed one another in frequent, if irregular, succession.

One of the most graphic and best recollected of this group of political events was the arrest of Mr. William O'Brien in Manchester, and his subsequent treatment whilst in the custody of the Chief Constable of that city in the palatial buildings known as the Town Hall. But what lent great point to this event was the halo that surrounded the prisoner and made him the hero of the hour with his countrymen and the political party to which he belonged. Mr. O'Brien had just previously escaped from the Court-house of Carrick-on-Suir, and this caused attention to be concentrated on him, as he was then a fugitive from justice in his native land. Towards the end of January, 1889, it had been announced, by means of advertisements in the Manchester newspapers, and by large placards extensively posted on the walls of that city, that Mr. O'Brien would address a meeting in the Hulme Town Hall on the 29th of January, the gathering being styled as an "indignation meeting against the Government of Lord Salisbury." The intense public excitement existing naturally led to the gathering of a large and excited crowd to see and hear the hero who was defying the British Government.

Acting under the instructions of the Chief Constable of Manchester (Mr. C. Malcolm Wood), I took a prominent part in the arrest of Mr. O'Brien at the meeting, and subsequently accompanied him to custody in Dublin. The following may be taken as absolutely authentic.

On the 29th January, 1889, I was called into the office of the Chief Constable, and instructed to take charge of a warrant which had been brought to Manchester from Ireland by one of the Head Constables of the Royal Irish Constabulary for the arrest of Mr. William O'Brien.

The Head Constable was accompanied by one of the Irish constables permanently stationed in Manchester. On asking these constables for a description of Mr. O'Brien, whom I had not previously seen, it turned out that the execution of the warrant had been entrusted to the hands of men who were totally unacquainted with the person of whom they were in search, and neither of the Irish officers could give the simple information I wanted. As the day wore on all sorts of rumours filled the air. It was said that Mr. O'Brien had arrived; that a band of armed Radicals and Irishmen had been organised to protect him; that there would be bloodshed if his arrest was attempted; and so on.

In the meantime I got the warrant endorsed by Mr. Headlam, the Stipendiary Magistrate, and the Chief Constable communicated with the Mayor, informing him that if the arrest took place in Manchester he had reason to believe that it would cause great excitement, and possibly disturbance. His Worship thereupon made arrangements to remain at the Town Hall in case he should be required. As Mr. O'Brien was unknown to any of us, there was nothing for it but to allow him to establish his own identity. At 5.30 p.m. I told off the detective staff, ordering them to proceed to the Hulme Town Hall, and obtain entrance by one of the private doors, without giving offence to any of the persons assembled. Even at that early hour Stretford Road, in which the hall is situate was packed by a rough and noisy crowd, and the adjacent streets were occupied by thousands of fiery spirits, who seemed more inclined for a row than a lecture. The utmost excitement prevailed.

About seven o'clock one of the detective officers was challenged by a well-known foreign gentleman of princely name, who at that time figured very prominently in the Socialist movement. He was one of those people who neglect their own affairs to attend to those of the community, who do not care one jot how their own particular business goes, provided they can keep themselves well before the public and have full scope to air their own peculiar notions for the regeneration of society at large. To accomplish this object they run about from morning till night, going through an immense amount of labour and fatigue. A man of this stamp is always ready to remove all nuisances (except himself), to remedy all local grievances, head all sorts of deputations, take the lead in all sorts of public movements; but you seldom see his name on a subscription list, or hear of him doing "good by stealth and blushing to find it fame!" The answer the officer gave this individual led him to come to discuss matters with me. He did not, however, learn much, and as I did not like his manner I followed him up the stairs from the basement of the Town Hall, and was just in time to hear him thus haranguing in the yard of the hall about 100 silly fellows who had no more sense than to listen to him-

"You must defend Mr. O'Brien at the cost of your lives. He must not be taken alive;" and so on.

Such was the language of this man, who was one of the shining lights of the Hulme Radical Club, the organisation which appeared to have control of the meeting. I hardly need add that this hater of princes took good care to keep his precious skin far enough away from any part of the hall where there was likely to be a *mêlée* during the evening, though he was exciting the crowd to violence in the manner I have described.

Turning on my heel, I said to the crowd, "I suppose you are aware that this person keeps a small shop in Stretford Road. He is not a wealthy man. Now, before you follow his instructions I would ask you to consider whether he is likely to pay for any damage that may be done; whether he will be able to free you from any punishment that you may bring upon yourselves; or whether he is even able to find money to provide counsel to defend him." "If Mr. O'Brien comes here to-night will you stop him?" asked the prince. "I don't know whether he is coming or not," he continued. "If he comes," I replied, "I will see him safely on to the platform, and no one shall interfere with him."

At the time this gentleman was advocating violence, I was the only officer in the hall (with the exception of Detective Officers Schofield, Hargraves, and Wilson, whom I had placed amongst the audience for the purpose of gathering information of any ruse that might be arranged for Mr. O'Brien's escape), the others being in the basement of the building, out of sight.

Soon after half-past seven a cab drove up to the front of the hall. A cry was raised that it contained Mr. O'Brien, and a great cheer was sent up by the crowd. Out of the cab jumped a man, muffled up, of a similar stature to the description given me of Mr. O'Brien, who was immediately surrounded by as rough and determined a crowd as I ever saw in my life, and he was hustled upstairs into the ante-room.

As I was perfectly well acquainted with the dodge, no one attempted to interfere with the muffled gentleman, and they had their trouble for nothing, whilst the air was filled with cries of "O'Brien!" "O'Brien!" "He has arrived!" I was standing by myself in the yard, leaning upon a hose-cart, when the gate was suddenly opened and a crowd rushed in, augmenting the number present to between two and three hundred. Mr. O'Brien and others came in this way, and were immediately surrounded by the great prince and his body guard, and pushed up the stairs into the ante-room. I could not help smiling at the great precautions taken, seeing that I was the only officer on the scene. Mr. O'Brien himself appeared to be very indignant at the treatment he received from his enthusiastic but inconsiderate supporters, and remonstrated with them. The ante-room, which was used as a committee-room, and from which there was access to the platform, was in possession of the organisers of the meeting, and they immediately proceeded to post a staff of "lambs" around the door to resist any effort on the part of the police to enter. These precautions were entirely uncalled for, as no one had any intention of entering at that time. I saw, however, that things were looking ugly, and that if the gentleman with the princely name and one or two others were to have their way there would be trouble. I therefore went into the basement, and after telling the officers that things were looking black, warned them to take no orders but from me direct, and to act altogether. I also despatched an officer for the Chief-Constable, but Mr. Malcolm Wood had already arrived in the hall.

After a conference with him I asked that the reserves should be called out, and in less than twenty minutes we had over four hundred officers and constables on the spot. Two hundred and fifty were brought in at the principal entrance to the hall, and formed in line on each side, and the doors were partially closed, so that only one person at a time could pass through their lines. One hundred and fifty police held a good front outside, with the hall in their rear, and with thirty on the landing I had sufficient force at my disposal to block every entrance in such a manner that no person could make an exit without my permission. I was sure that Mr. O'Brien was in the hall, and that he was now safely in the trap. Soon afterwards I was spoken to by two members of the Committee, both Justices of the Peace, and a truce was about to be proclaimed, on condition that Mr. O'Brien should surrender himself at the close of the meeting. To arrange this matter I was invited to enter the ante-room. As I proceeded thither with the two gentlemen referred to, with the object of negotiating the matter, a rush was made by the "lambs" who protected the door. I was seized by some of the "gentlemen" from behind, and surrounded by others. Whilst being thus rushed from the scene, I received a good kicking, of which my shins bore the marks for many a day. Nevertheless, I kept myself cool. To have called for the aid of the force at that time, in the excited state of the meeting, would probably have occasioned a riot, so I acted on the principle that he who waits may win. Statements were freely made that blood would be shed before Mr. O'Brien should be taken, and that he was protected by forty men armed with revolvers.

Upon this the Chief Constable thought proper to send for Mr. Jacob Bright, M.P., who was the principal speaker at the meeting, and told him that he held a warrant for the arrest of Mr. O'Brien, that the hall was filled with police, and that it was impossible for Mr. O'Brien to escape. He then pointed out that in the temper of the meeting there was great danger of a riot and bloodshed, and to save any loss of life he asked him to see Mr. O'Brien, and get to know whether he would consent to surrender peaceably. Mr. Bright, who was greatly excited, consented to see Mr. O'Brien, and soon returned with the message that Mr. O'Brien would make no terms with anyone. "Very well then," said the Chief Constable, "you must take the responsibility of what occurs," and Mr. Bright returned to the platform. War being now declared, we began to prepare for the capture in earnest. I made sure that no ladder was prepared for the purpose of aiding Mr. O'Brien's escape by the window of the ante-room, which appeared our only weak spot, and then returned to a position in the corridor where I could see all that was going on in the hall through the open doorway. Whilst standing here for a time, some of those present amused themselves by jeering at me through the glass window of a door of the ante-room, asking me, "Have you got him?" "Wouldn't you like him?" "Does your mother know you're out?" etc. Showing me bacon, they placed themselves in all kinds of ignoble attitudes. Whilst, however, I was their target for ridicule twenty detectives, whom I had placed in the corridor, had instructions from me to keep pressing the "lambs" who filled the corridor, and whilst I was attracting the attention of the "lambs" the officers were steadily gaining ground by acting in concert, without raising a hand, until the "lambs" were all forced downstairs and we were left in sole possession of the corridor. A disaster befell them. They were not content with the meeting inside, and it occurred to one that the great crowd outside could be worked up to a higher pitch of excitement, and that it would be a splendid opportunity for some of the stump orators, who were bursting with enthusiasm, to air their eloquence. For this purpose the door of the ante-room was opened sufficiently wide to allow one of these gentlemen to pass, when Detective Sergeant Goodwin (who looks anything but a detective officer) by my orders slipped into the room, upon which they commenced to pull him about, with the intention of turning him out, tearing his clothes, and otherwise ill-using him. Whilst they were thus engaged I rushed into the room, followed by a number of detective officers whom I had ready, in expectation of such an occurrence. As those inside immediately tried to shut the door the poor orator was jammed between the door and the post, and I fear all the eloquence was well-nigh crushed out of him. We had, however, no time to make inquiry on that subject. He was a sufficient barrier to prevent the door being closed, and we soon carried the room. These fellows now found out that there were two sides to a ladder. The officers immediately began to clear the room, and, considering all they had to put up with, and remembering the manner in which they had heard me treated shortly before, the "chucking out" process was perhaps not so gentle as might have been desired. After the occupants of the room had been ejected they were quickly run through a line of officers into the street, where they found themselves, without any necessity of asking their mothers if they knew they were out. Their bombast at once collapsed, and the woebegone looks of the valiant body guard, who had so lately been talking of "blood and thunder," were not a little amusing. The only means of escape for Mr. O'Brien was now cut off, and we had full admission to the platform from the rear at anytime we thought proper to use it; whilst we had a large body of men ready to storm it in front if that movement became necessary. Mr. O'Brien mounted the platform at the close of Mr. Bright's speech amidst a tempest of applause, and at once identified himself by announcing that he was William O'Brien, the escaped prisoner, from Carrick. We now knew our man. With our 400 drilled men, properly led and all acting in unison, we could have cleared the hall in a few minutes; but the Chief Constable, who felt responsible for the safety of the city, gave distinct orders that nothing should be done to provoke disorder, and that to avoid riot and bloodshed the meeting must be allowed to terminate before any attempt was made to effect the arrest.

The end, however, soon came without any violence on the part of the police; but, as we had been defied, I got upon the platform and faced the meeting. At the conclusion of Mr. O'Brien's speech an excited crowd immediately made a dash for the platform, scrambling over the reporters' tables.

The tables, chairs, forms, and other articles were soon overthrown, and the hero of the night was quickly surrounded by an excited and angry crowd, some threatening to dislocate his arms by shaking them, others prepared "to do and die" rather than allow him to be taken. How insignificant such an opposition must have been to a number of trained men acting together under authorised leaders must have been apparent to many of these people in their calmer moments; but the action of the "defenders" only hastened the end which they wished to put off. Mr. O'Brien was being pulled about by his excited friends, and it was soon evident that if something was not done he would be overpowered, notwithstanding their good intentions. I beckoned from the platform to the Chief Constable, who at once joined me, accompanied by a number of detectives. He was immediately struck on the chest and knocked backwards off the platform, carrying in his fall four of the detective officers who were following him up. I immediately struck the man who had committed the assault a violent blow on the side of the head, which sent him after the officers. The platform stands about four feet above the level of the floor, and it was not a gentle fall. Fortunately the attack upon the Chief Constable was not seen by the main body of the police; but it was difficult to restrain those who did witness it. A little space was cleared, and the Chief Constable again ascended the platform.

I immediately made my way across the platform to Mr. O'Brien, who was in a fainting condition, surrounded by an excited crowd of friends.

Having reached him I assisted him along the platform, down the steps, and into the ante-room, and the reader may readily imagine what a scene of excitement followed. It became a question of who was to hold the fort. A general "chucking-out" match was at once in full force, and we soon cleared the room.

Mr. O'Brien then asked to see the warrant, and on its being shown him he surrendered without more ado. In fact there was no option for him. By this time the crowd outside had attained enormous proportions, and the question was, "How is Mr. O'Brien to be conveyed to the Town Hall?" To take a cab meant its being overturned, an attempt at rescue, and lives probably lost. The Chief Constable therefore decided to form his men into a square, place Mr. O'Brien in the midst of them, and walk with him to the Town Hall. This was done, and we were followed all the way by an excited and angry crowd, amongst which there were very many of Manchester's best citizens, and a portion of the crowd singing, "He's a jolly good fellow," etc. The Chief Constable drew the attention of Mr. O'Brien to the harmony which existed between the police and the people, and the fact caused Mr. O'Brien to laugh heartily.

Immediately after the arrest, the Chief Constable telegraphed to Ireland for orders respecting Mr. O'Brien, and received a reply desiring that he should be sent on to Dublin by the first available boat. I was instructed to see this duty safely accomplished. As it was extremely desirable, in the heated state of political opinion which had been aroused, to prevent a crowd from assembling on our route, it was given out that Mr. O'Brien would be taken to Minshull Street Police Court the next morning at ten o'clock; but there was no necessity to do this, as the warrant under which he had been arrested was one for commitment to gaol. The Chief Constable arranged with the London and North-Western Railway Company to stop the 9.40 train from Manchester to Holyhead, at Ordsall Lane Station, and twenty minutes before the hour at which the crowd expected to have their curiosity gratified at Minshull Street, three Manchester Detectives, two Head Constables of the Royal Irish Constabulary, Mr. O'Brien, and I were *en route* for Kingstown.

On the way, I had the pleasure of telling Mr. O'Brien many little incidents of my experience of Irish affairs. With these he was very much amused, and my companion was a pleasant and agreeable man, bearing no resemblance to the excited politician, agitator, and demagogue of whom I had heard. We had a pleasant journey until Kingstown was reached, when the orders carried into effect were something very different from what we were accustomed to in

Manchester. We first got into a railway carriage, then out at the opposite door, to enter a brougham in which we were driven to Kingsbridge Station. There we had to wait about three hours, during which time Mr. O'Brien was visited by a large number of his friends.

Mr. Timothy Healy, M.P., who was proceeding to Carrick, for the purpose of conducting legal proceedings in connection with the case, arrived on the scene about half-an-hour before the train started, and asked that he might be allowed to accompany Mr. O'Brien on the journey, as it was impossible for him to receive proper instructions whilst waiting at the station.

On Mr. Healy speaking to the Head Constable who had come with us from Manchester, he was referred to another Head Constable in charge of the guard, and he, on being asked, hesitated to grant the request. Thus each of the constables declined to accept the responsibility. This angered Mr. O'Brien's friends, whereupon I tried to "throw oil on the troubled waters." Taking Mr. Healy by the arm, I walked to where the Head Constable in charge of the guard was stationed, and after fully discussing the question with him, I succeeded in persuading him that the only way to preserve the temper of Mr. O'Brien's friends was to allow Mr. Healy to go with him in the carriage, which was eventually done.

On the train starting, Mr. O'Brien came to the window of the carriage and requested me to approach him, when, to the great astonishment of the crowd, he publicly thanked me and the Manchester Police for our kindness to him. And so the train steamed away amidst the ringing cheers of the thousands of people who had assembled on the platform, amongst whom were the Lord Mayor, the High Sheriff of Dublin, and many Members of Parliament.

17

A QUEER CUSTOMER

Aracecourse is the centre of demoralisation in a neighbourhood for miles around, and draws to it, as if by magnetic force, the scampdom of the country.

Having been told off for duty at Lincoln Races, I stood one evening after the racing was over on the platform of the railway station, watching the people taking their departure, when I noticed a man acting in a very suspicious manner. He pushed along with the crowd to the carriage doors, raising his arms as he did so to the level of the vest pockets of the persons against whom he was pressing, but he never entered any of the carriages. At length he left the station hurriedly and made off down the middle of the street at a considerable speed. I at once gave chase, and after some time came up with him; but as he resisted, I dragged him on to the footpath, and then into an earthenware dealer's shop close at hand. Here a struggle took place, and as we both fell to the floor, each fighting to be uppermost in the midst of the crockery ware, a succession of crashes - basins, bowls, and other utensils being kicked about in all directions -

soon brought the proprietors into the shop from the living apartment behind. These happened to be an old couple; and as they stood behind the counter with uplifted hands, and without the power of speech, watching the two strange men fighting on the floor in the midst of their property, the amazement depicted upon their countenances may be better imagined than described. I managed at length to get the "snaps" on my prisoner, and after mollifying the old people and informing them that I was a police officer, I started with my man for the police station. After proceeding for some distance he assured me that I had made a mistake, and threatened me with the pains and penalties usual in such cases. Finding, however, that this would not act, he invited me to settle the matter over some oysters and brandy. As I declined all his invitations he now had recourse to another move which, though it amused, rather than surprised me, and was afterwards a source of some trouble to the Lincoln authorities. As we passed along towards the station he suddenly assumed a very erect position, threw his hands by his sides, and uttered an exclamation something like "whir, whir, whir, whir!" evidently pretending to be silly and dumb.Arrived at the station, nothing could be got from him in answer to any question but, "whir, whir, whir, whir!" Many efforts were made to induce him to speak, a can of water even being poured on his head; but they all proved useless, the only articulation that could be got from him being "whir, whir, whir, whir!" The next morning when I appeared against him before the magistrate he played the same antics; nothing could be got from him but the eternal, "whir, whir, whir, whir." But this stood him in little stead, for he was sentenced to three months' imprisonment.

At this time the city of Lincoln boasted of a gaol, which was officered by a governor, a chief warder, and three assistant warders. Their duties were but light, as they had only five prisoners to look after. When, however, they got possession of their new prisoner matters changed with them. He carried on so dreadfully with his "whir, whir, whir, whir!" and acted the part of a lunatic so well, that he had to be looked after night and day, and not only found employment for the whole of the officials, but the prisoners besides. It is needless to say that the latter greatly enjoyed the fun. So well did he act his part, and such inconveniences did he cause, that the visiting justices of the city of Lincoln wrote to the Home Secretary, laying the case before him and asking what they were to do with the prisoner. The Home Secretary communicated with me asking if I was sure I had heard the man speak. As I could only answer in the affirmative, relating the incidents connected with his arrest, not forgetting the brandy and oyster episode, the Lincoln officials were obliged to keep their troublesome prisoner a little longer.

After he had served about two months of his sentence he startled his keepers one morning by suddenly finding his tongue. He wanted to know where he was and what he had been doing; but on the governor being summoned, he admitted that he had been acting, and thought he had done it very well. He had got tired, however, of the play, as it did not bring about the end he had in view, and had become too troublesome.

Further inquiries proved him to be the convict who, having been convicted of a very extensive jeweller's shop robbery, a violin box containing a set of burglar's tools having been found in his possession, carried on a similar deception which caused him to be sent to Broadmoor Lunatic Asylum, from which he managed to escape.

18

"FLYING GIBB"

A TROUBLESOME CUSTOMER

At the time I commenced duty as a detective, burglaries were very numerous, scarcely a day passing without one or more being reported. I was one of the officers told off to deal with this particular class of crime. My inquiries led me to notice a gang of young thieves who had gained some notoriety in the neighbourhood of Chorlton-upon-Medlock. They were usually to be seen in groups standing about the end of Grey Street, Brook Street, from noon till late on in the afternoon, the ages of these young aspirants to a criminal career ranging from 17 to 22 years. Some of the gang followed regular employment, but the greater part of them were content with picking up odd jobs, and on Sundays a general assembly of the lot usually took place, to the great annoyance of the neighbourhood.

Their little visits to prison, and attendance at trotting matches, foot-races, dog-races, and other such low amusements, brought them into contact with older and more experienced criminals. They thus became hardened in crime.

The following sketch will give the reader a good idea of the tricks of this school:-

About the year 1868, "Flying Gibb" was arrested for stealing from the person at Old Trafford Steeplechases, but after a remand was discharged. Soon after, he was again caught and sentenced to fourteen days' imprisonment for stealing a tame rabbit. On his release he returned to work for a short time; but as honest employment was too monotonous for Gibb, he soon blossomed into a very dangerous and expert thief.

One morning a report came to the office that a jeweller's shop in Stretford Road had been robbed by someone reaching over the counter, sliding back the window, and taking a tray containing twelve gold watches. We were at once set to work, and a visit was paid to Bob McFarlane's, who at this time kept a beerhouse in the neighbourhood of Charter Street. On two officers entering the house, Gibb, a lady friend, and two others were in the kitchen. As soon as he saw them, Gibb ran upstairs, dropped through the bedroom window, and got clear away with nine of the watches in his possession. His lady friend, Mary Ann Parr, put two of the watches inside a roller towel; but the watches being found she was arrested and sentenced to six months' imprisonment.

Gibbs was afterwards met at the Southport Railway Station during an agricultural show. He was taken into custody by Inspector Clayton, and as they were quietly crossing the line to get to the Police Station, Gibb suddenly turned round, tripped up the inspector - who was one of the officers who had made the visit to McFarlane's beerhouse, and had arrested his female accomplice - and making off succeeded in escaping him a second time.

Some time afterwards a jeweller's shop was broken into

in Preston, and a very large quantity of jewellery stolen. Three persons were arrested for it, one being a tradesman in the town, who was charged with receiving a portion of the property knowing it to have been stolen, and two others, one of them belonging to Gibb's gang. This led to inquiries about Gibb, and a telegram was received by the Chief Constable of Manchester to the following effect: "Wanted here for jeweller's shop burglary, Gibb or Gibbs, known to your Sergeant Caminada. Arrest. Very important."

No trace, however, was to be got of Gibb. The case went for trial, and the three men were convicted. The tradesman, who had previously served twelve months' imprisonment in this city, and who was afraid of being sent to penal servitude, was sentenced to twelve months' imprisonment, and ordered to pay the whole costs of the trial out of his own estate. Gibbs afterwards put in an appearance, but the Preston police could not make out a case against him.

One Sunday night Inspector Schofield was passing along Deansgate when he came to a crowd of persons watching two women fighting in their midst. He was endeavouring to separate them when Gibb, who was present, snatched the inspector's stick out of his hand, struck him a violent blow with it on the head, which felled him to the ground, and once more took to his heels.

I was very anxious to meet with Gibb, when a report came from the Bolton police asking for his arrest on suspicion of having stolen a cash-box containing a large sum of money. Soon afterwards I met Gibb, about four o'clock one afternoon, coming out of the Grecian Inn, a house at that time situated near Peter Street, Deansgate, and visited by loose characters, but afterwards pulled down for the widening of the street.

"Well, James," I said, "how are you? I shall require your

presence for a short time at the Detective Office," and at once seized hold of him. His friends, scenting danger, were very anxious to know what he was required for. Seeing that there was some likelihood of a rescue I at once clenched Gibb with both my arms round him, so that the whole weight of both of us would have to be dealt with, when a uniform sergeant came to my assistance and a very tough struggle took place. The sergeant, who was a man advanced in years, and was not cut out for a row of this kind, was soon *hors de combat*, and I soon had Gibb to myself. I got him as far as John Dalton Street when another tough struggle took place. At length I got him to the corner of St James's Square and here he tripped me up, getting the larger portion of my body over the cellar railing, and throwing the whole weight of his body upon me endeavoured to force me, head fore-most, into the area, a fall of about eighteen feet. A firm grip, however, round his neck with the knuckle of my fists well into his throat caused him to slacken a little in his attempt, and another struggle took place in which we were both soon rolling on the ground. A little progress was made towards the Detective Office, and after another scuffle I managed to get the "snaps" on Gibb. But he was not done for yet. He now made another desperate effort for liberty. He wrenched the "snaps" off his wrist and I struck him several blows. Fighting our way towards the Detective Office, then in the old Town Hall, we both went down in Cross Street in the midst of a large puddle of water. The rain was coming down in torrents at the time, and the soughs being stopped, as generally happens after dry weather, large pools of water were formed in different places. Through one of these we fought and rolled, until at last I dragged him into the Detective Office. What with mud, wet, and torn clothing we both presented a nice spectacle. But no sooner had I got Gibb in the office than he fell on the floor like one dead, and fainted away. On his recovery he complained that his shoulder was hurt - but he was at last secured.

He was taken before the Court the next morning and sentenced to three months' imprisonment for the assault on Inspector Schofield, 10s. 6d. and costs for the assault upon me, and ordered to pay the cost of the damage done to my clothing. The Bolton police had not sufficient evidence to convict him for the jewellery robbery.

After his release from prison Gibb formed the acquaintance of a Manchester tradesman, who carried on the business of a painter in the centre of the city, to which he added that of a "fence," or a buyer of stolen property. This man was a very useful friend to the "cracksmen" of the period, as he was able to "put them up" to jobs in those houses to which he obtained admittance in the ordinary course of his business. The man was known to me, for some time before I had apprehended him on the Infirmary Esplanade for loitering with the intent to commit a felony, for which he was sentenced to a month's imprisonment.

One morning I noticed these two gentlemen leaving the shop of Messrs. Worthington and Myers, pawnbrokers, Deansgate, and one of them was busy tearing up a piece of paper. A bit dropped on to the pavement, and as they passed on I picked it up and found that it contained the number of a pawnbroker's duplicate. Inquiries elicited the fact that it related to a watch which had just been pledged. Taking the number and description of the article I proceeded to the Detective Office, where I found that the report of a watch robbery had been sent in, committed by two men under the following circumstances:-

The manager of the King's Head, a public-house, which formerly stood at the corner of Lower Mosley Street and

Windmill Street - now the site of Central Station - was entering the premises when his watch-guard became entangled with the handle of the door, and his watch was dragged out of his vest pocket and the glass broken. He at once sent the watch to Mr. Longworth's, a jeweller, across the road, to be repaired.

Gibb, and "Flash Bob," as his companion was called, were both in the public house at the time, saw all that happened, and after sympathising with the manager, departed. Before leaving the neighbourhood, however, they stepped across the street into Mr. Longworth's shop, and informed him that the manager of the King's Head had sent them for his watch. Mr. Longworth, however, refused to give it up. But, notwithstanding his vigilance, when they had gone away he found that they had taken with them a watch that had been left to be repaired by Sir James Watts' coachman. The description of this watch answered to the one that these two men had pawned.

I then set out to find the clever gentlemen. But all my searching was of no avail, until one night I and another officer met the men together with "Harriet the Maid" and Mary Ann Parr, in a street close by London Road Railway Station. I at once seized Bob, and my colleagues got hold of Gibb, when the women became very noisy and violent. I had not proceeded far with my prisoner when I was made aware that a scuffle was going on between Gibb and my colleague. Gibb was making another bold fight for liberty, and called out to my prisoner to draw his knife and let me have it. In the end my colleague, finding himself overpowered, called for assistance, and leaving my prisoner I rushed to his aid. Finding that he had got too great a start to be overtaken, I again turned my attention to Bob, who had taken to his heels. After an exciting chase, I came up with him, and we lodged him safely in the Detective Office. The following day he was committed to the Sessions, and sentenced to three months' imprisonment.

After this Gibb was not heard of for about eighteen months, when I got news that he had returned to the city. I at once went in search of him. Ascertaining that he had commenced to work, I turned out at 4.30 a.m. to see if I could meet with him. One morning I had left Sergeant Thompson at the corner of Rusholme Road, and was walking down one of the streets in the neighbourhood, when a window was raised, and a voice called out asking what the time was? A girl, who was passing, answered that it was "a quarter past five," and the window was again closed. I at once recognised the voice as that of Gibb, and stepping into a passage I soon had the satisfaction of seeing the room lit up, and the shadow of my old acquaintance, which I immediately recognised, thrown upon the blind.

Returning to my colleague I told him of my success. It was arranged that he should wait at the end of the street, and that the moment I put my hands upon Gibb, I would call to him, when he was to rush to my assistance.

The door of the house in which this desperate character lived, had an elevation of five steps from the footpath, and a struggle on the top might have been far from pleasant. I therefore determined, if possible, to take Gibb by surprise. About 5.30 the light left the bedroom, and I took my stand upon the top step. I heard the key turned in the lock, and the moment the door was opened, I dashed in, seized my man, dragged him down the steps into the street, called out "Jack," and Thompson came to my assistance. We hurried Gibb along with such haste down Brook Street that we reached the canal bridge in Princess Street before Gibb appeared to have recovered from the surprise of this sudden attack.

Having recovered his presence of mind, and taken in the situation, he requested us to "loose him" and he would go quietly. Finding, however, that this did not act, he attempted to shuffle himself loose, and said that I was hurting his arm. I told him, however, that he had better not let us have any more of his nonsense or we might have a reckoning. Seeing that it was useless to try on any more of his old games, he went quietly to the Detective Office. He was afterwards sentenced at the City Sessions to six months' imprisonment for the larceny and the assault.

I again lost sight of Gibb for some time, when a description was circulated of three men who had been committed for trial for a very daring hotel robbery, at Middlesborough, and who had also used great violence to the police on their arrest. These men had been in Northallerton gaol for six weeks, and refused to be photographed, though they had been put on punishment diet, which was bread and water, for nearly the whole of that period. This naturally made the authorities suspicious that they were old offenders. As they refused to give way, the officials at the prison communicated with the police in various towns, and I was ordered to visit the prison and see if I could identify them. I at once recognised them as my old friend Gibb, "The Chinaman," and "Scotch Johnny." At the following Sessions I proved previous convictions, when they were sentenced to various terms of imprisonment, Gibb getting nine months, and seven years' police supervision.

Immediately on his release he was again apprehended, and sent to the same prison to await his trial for an hotel robbery at Stockton during the races, for which he was afterwards sentenced to fifteen months' imprisonment and a renewal of the supervision.

Some time after his discharge I met him at the Chichester Railway Station, among a gang of racecourse thieves, of which some account is given in another part of my *Reminiscences*, when I took him into custody for not having reported himself according to the terms of his last sentence. I took him before the city magistrates; but their clerk said it was a county case, and would have to be adjudicated upon by the county justices. I took him across the street to the County Police Court; but the clerk for the county magistrates ruled that it was a city case. So back we went to the City Court, who again sent us to the County Court. After this game of shuttlecock had gone on for some time, the clerk to the county magistrates said the case should be decided on the following Monday.

Having to wait over the week-end, I went down to Portsmouth to view the wreck of the Eurydice, one of Her Majesty's training ships, which had gone down during a squall of wind off Ventnor, Isle of Wight, while returning from the West Indies with 323 men on board, two only of whom were saved, most of the men being asleep at the time. The wreck, when I visited it, was being prepared for the inspection of His Royal Highness the Prince of Wales, which was to take place the following day.

I returned to Chichester on the Monday morning, and as I arrived the clerk to the county justices, who were to adjudicate upon my case, was leaving the town with the Bishop of the diocese. It appeared that, besides being clerk to the magistrates, he was the secretary of his lordship, who required his services elsewhere that morning. As the magistrates were unable to adjudicate upon the case without the assistance of their clerk, justice had to play second fiddle to the Bishop's convenience, to the benefit of Gibb, who once more got his freedom.

The manner in which the police business of the city of Chichester was conducted was not very creditable to the authorities. When it was necessary to prove from the *Police Gazette* that Gibb was wanted, it turned out that the numbers, instead of being properly filed, were lying upstairs in the chief constable's house unopened! As they had arrived they had been thrown on one side without even the wrappers having been taken off, and it was necessary to open each one and examine it before we could find what we required. It was evident that the duties of the police in this district were light, and that they were not anxious to make them any heavier except, perhaps in the matter of drawing their salaries. It would have been a splendid place for criminals to vegetate in, had it not been for the periodical incursions of the police from other parts of the country.

Gibb, I may say, has since developed into a Continental thief, and keeps a place of business not far from Charing Cross, London, from which he makes excursions to all parts of the Continent in the pursuit of his old business.

19

FRAUDS ON UNEMPLOYED GIRLS

There are few frauds of a worse kind than those by which respectable girls are induced to leave their homes. Finding themselves destitute among strangers they become an easy prey to the wily seducer. In May, 1893, the following advertisement appeared in a London newspaper:-

"YOUNG LADY REQUIRED FOR SHOW-ROOM. First-class trade. Manchester. Salary £60 limit; if not experienced considerably less given. Live in house. Write Alphonse et Cie, 81, Bury New Road, Manchester."

THIS BROUGHT many replies from young ladies anxiously seeking employment, and in response they each received a letter to the following effect:-

"ALPHONSE, Redfern et Cie.

"Robes, Modes, Lingerie, et Corsets.

"Manchester, May 17, 1893.

"MADAM,

"Please send photo by return showing style of figure, if full or slim; also state age and salary required. We should only wish you to give a month; you would have to dress well, however, both as regards gown and underwear. Messrs. A. and R. are establishing themselves in Manchester from Paris, in first-class style, and are very particular about their staff. They must have ladies in their show-rooms who will do credit to their establishment as regards appearances, etc. The hours are from 9 to 6.45, and 2 o'clock on Saturdays. You will live in of course.

"I am, madam,

"Yours faithfully,

"M. E. (For Alphonse et Cie)

"Reply to 81, Bury New Road, which is the manager's address until the firm opens."

THE BAIT WAS SO TEMPTING that many young ladies sent their photographs, with other particulars about themselves, and, in reply, received a letter headed "Alphonse et Cie" - "Opening Deansgate, Manchester." After acknowledging the receipt of the photograph, the writer would inform some of the applicants that their "bust would no doubt be improved by our corsets." Others would require "a French-made gown, cut by a man, and corsets and shoes to suit their appearance;" but all were told that they had better be prepared to come over, if, after talking it over with the manageress, the writer requested them to do so.

Further correspondence would necessarily take place. In due course the applicants would be informed that they would probably "suit;" but if they came over they would have to pay their own railway fare, "and there would be the expense of a gown (cash with order)," and "they would have to assist with getting the premises and house ready." "The usual showroom costume" was "black satin with train," and the applicant could get it herself if she thought proper; but then, "perhaps the manageress would let her have it for almost a nominal figure, if she was satisfied with other things." Later this "nominal figure" would resolve itself into "about £4 4s. 0d., cash with order, although it will stand in our books about seven; but as we should charge our customers ten guineas for a similar one, no doubt they have asked you the same elsewhere." "The costume" was "the usual one worn in the Paris and West End showrooms, made in the latest Parisian mode."

Should the terms be complained of, "the manager" was fully equal to the occasion - they were not those of the firm, but were those offered by more than enough ladies to fill the vacancies, therefore in justice to his firm the manager could not take them on any other. Then again, "The manager thought of going to London, but the most suitable of the applicants were staying with their friends in the country, and Manchester was more convenient for them; so if he went to London it would not help them." "The manager," the applicants were informed, was staying at Grafton Street, near Whitworth Park, which is about half-an-hour's walk from Deansgate (where the shop was to be opened); but this would be too far, and too expensive for the staff, except as a temporary arrangement; therefore a house nearer to the business would be arranged for them. There were to be two ladies to every bedroom, but each to have "separate beds;"

food was to "be good and plentiful" and the manager would arrange for the laundry. Add to this, that their appearance would be greatly improved by "a French made gown, cut by a man," with corset and shoes to match, and a good salary to be paid monthly, in the bargain, and what young lady would not cast longing eyes on such an earthly paradise?

Can it be wondered at that the tempting bait took, and that many young ladies came over to Manchester, paying their own fares, in addition to the four guineas for the "French gown to be cut by a man" which was to so greatly improve their appearance?

Three of these young ladies, who were supposed to be engaged at salaries ranging from £25 to £45 per annum, he took to a boarding-house in Bury New Road.

As to their terms of engagement, the following may be taken as a specimen:-

"ALPHONSE REDFERN ET CIE,

   "Robes, Modes, Lingerie, et Corsets,

   "Opening Deansgate, Manchester, June, 1st week, 1893,

   "May, 27, 1893.

"MADAM,-

"With reference to your application, after to-day's personal interview I agree to engage you for Messrs. Alphonse Redfern's showrooms at above address, on the following terms, namely: That you pay your fare to Manchester; that you order a gown to wear in business, paying for the same on ordering; that you give a week to assist in the preparations for opening; and that your salary be £20 for the first six months, and if we are satisfied to be

£25 for the second. The usual notice on either side to be given in case of leaving.

"I AM,

"Yours faithfully,
"ALPHONSE REDFERN."

HE INFORMED these young people that he was the nephew of Mr. Redfern, head of the well known firm of Redfern Limited, of Paris, with branches in London and other places, and told them that the Manchester premises were to be opened on the eighth of June, and took some of them to the door of Grosvenor Chambers, Deansgate, where he said the business was to be carried on. One of these girls he employed in writing letters at his dictation to young ladies respecting engagements; another he sent out to look out for a suitable house as a home for the lady assistants, rent not to exceed £42; and the third was engaged in obtaining catalogues and estimates for the furnishing of this house.

On his way down Bury New Road with the first of these young ladies, a day or two after her arrival, the supposed Mr. Redfern pointed out a photographer's shop, in the windows of which were a number of photographs of actors and actresses, and said that as there would be a number of fancy dresses at his establishment, it would be necessary for his assistants to put them on for ladies to see. After supper the same evening he said it would be requisite for him to measure her for the costume for which she had paid, and that it would be necessary for her to take off her dress for the purpose, stating that all the measurements for costumes in Paris were taken by men. She complied with his request, and after measuring her for the costume he proceeded to measure her for a fancy dress round the ankle, the calf, and above the knee. The young lady complained and said she thought the latter was unnecessary, upon which Mr. Alphonse said he could not take proper measurements unless she removed her _____, which the young lady refused to do, and he had to be content with them as taken. He then asked her to make arrangements with one of the other young ladies to have the measurements taken in the way he suggested.

This second young lady, who had never been away from home before, was to be put into the showroom department and wear a fancy costume, which would not come below the knee. When she arrived she went to Grafton Street, where she found the supposed manager with the young lady, to whom he was dictating letters. After receiving her four guineas, he sent the letter writer away, saying that he would accompany the new arrival to Bury New Road himself. When the two were alone he said he would have to take the measurement for her fancy costume, and measured her bust, waist, and legs to the knee. He was about to measure the knee when the lady drew back and objected, as there was no one present; upon which he said that it was very unpleasant, but as his manageress had not arrived from Paris he was obliged to do it. She refused, however, to let him proceed with the measurement at the time. On the following day, at Bury New Road, after some conversation with the first young lady who had been measured, at his request she took off her dress, and, after measuring her round the bust and chest, he said it would be necessary for him to measure round her ankle and to take the length of her foot. On putting out her foot for him to get the measurement, whilst he was kneeling on the ground after taking the measurement of her ankle, he committed an indecent assault. Upon this she ran out of the room, and told the third lady what had occurred. This aroused the suspicions of this lady, who was twenty-six years of age, and, after making some inquiries, she brought the young lady who had been indecently assaulted to the Detective Office.

Inspector Hargreaves and I accompanied them to Bury New Road, and saw the prisoner, who gave me his name as Alphonse Redfern. On asking him if he had anything to show that he was acting for Messrs. Redfern, of London and Paris, he said that he was Mr. Redfern's nephew. As he could give me no references I took him into custody, and on searching him I found £5 10s. in his possession. I asked him what he had done with the twelve guineas he had received from the three ladies, and he then asked, if they received the money back would the prosecution be allowed to drop? In reply, I told him that he would be charged with procuring the girls for immoral purposes, and he said, "Don't charge me with that." Whilst searching him I found some papers, and he said that there were two £5 notes amongst them. As I could not find them, and as it was very evident that a gentleman of this kind would not be very particular about preferring a charge against the police, I requested him to point them out; but, as he could not do so, he at length accounted for their absence by saying that he had lost some money. I then took him to the Detective Office and charged him with obtaining money by false pretences, with an indecent assault, and with endeavouring to procure the girls for immoral purposes. His only reply was, "I am not so bad as you think I am."

Evidence was produced to show that he was in no way connected with "Redfern's Limited," who had already a branch established in Manchester, or with any of the family composing the firm; that it was not usual for the firm, though they supplied their assistants with dresses, to require them to pay for such; nor was it usual in the trade to measure assistants for underclothing.

The prisoner was sent for trial at the June Sessions, 1893 (Mr. Overend Evans prosecuted on behalf of the Crown), when he pleaded "Not guilty." After a patient trial, the jury found him guilty of both false pretences and indecent assault, and he was sentenced to twelve months' imprisonment on the first charge, and six months' imprisonment on the second charge, the sentences to run concurrently.

Nine or ten other girls, whom we had to send home, came in the same way as the three young ladies, and had not the prisoner been interfered with, it was probably his intention to get the girls abroad under the pretence of sending them to the Paris house for immoral purposes.

On his discharge from prison, he was re-arrested for offences committed in London, and was sentenced to 10 months' imprisonment. He was also wanted by the police elsewhere.

20

A CLEVER FORGER

THE HISTORY OF A NOTED CASE

On the 2nd of November, 1886, a man calling himself Arthur Foster, *alias* Walter Nicholls, *alias* William Cromley, *alias* Frank Falkland, but whose real name was W. G__, and who was in the employment of a solicitor at Birmingham as clerk, absconded with £5,200, which he had obtained from a client of his employer's by forging the endorsements on deeds, letters of credit, and other documents. The fraud was carried out with great skill. The man had previous to the forgery informed the client in London in his master's name that a "confidential man" would wait upon him on a certain day to receive the money. From the time of his leaving London no trace of his whereabouts could be discovered. A reward of £200 was offered for the detection of Foster, who, it appeared, had a noted career.

He had been convicted of embezzlement at Liverpool, in February, 1874, in the name of Frank Falkland, and sentenced to 18 months' hard labour. He was again convicted at the same place, on the 6th of December, 1876, on a charge of forgery, and sentenced to ten years' penal servitude. He was liberated on the 17th of February, 1885, on a ticket-of-leave, and soon afterwards became a newspaper reporter at Shrewsbury, remaining there till June, 1886, when he entered the service of Mr. Bradley, solicitor, of Birmingham, as shorthand writer. He absconded from this employment after committing the forgeries on the 2nd of November following. The police notice offering the reward contained a wood-cut of Foster, with a description of his person, and a statement to the effect that the reward would be paid "to any person giving such information as should lead to the apprehension and conviction of Foster, and the recovery of the money, or a lesser sum in proportion to the amount recovered." It was stated that £50 would be given "for the apprehension and conviction, in the event of no money being recovered."

It was quite evident that the runaway was no ordinary criminal, not only from the care with which he had planned and carried out the forgeries, but from the manner in which he had obtained the situation by means of false characters.

It appeared that having answered an advertisement of Mr. Bradley for a shorthand clerk, and having been asked for references, he had given the names and addresses of a solicitor at Shrewsbury, and another at Castle Fields. From these in due course Mr. Bradley received replies - one stating that Foster had been in the writer's office for over eight years; that he had risen to be general manager of the office; that his duty was "to look after the bookkeeping, common law, bankruptcy and county court practice;" and that he had left of his own accord, having given his employer perfect satisfaction. He had always been found "thoroughly honest, trustworthy, sober, and attentive to business." The other reference spoke of Foster as being a "straightforward, steady, conscientious man," and said "it was through no fault of his own that he had not risen to a better position in life, having had several pecuniary losses, in addition to more than an ordinary man's share of domestic affliction."

These letters were written on paper with printed headings, the name of the solicitor appearing in the first one within a garter in the left hand corner. No suspicion seems to have been entertained as to their *bona fides* until the case got into the papers, when the following letter received by Mr. Bradley threw some light upon the manner in which Foster had gone about his business:-

10th November, 1886.
Shrewsbury.

S<small>IR</small>, — My attention has been called to a paragraph in the *Birmingham Post*, in which the name of a Mr. __, solicitor, Shrewsbury, is mentioned. I beg to say that I never received a letter from you, or wrote one to you. My office has been for many years at 75, __ __, Shrewsbury, and my residence at __. I am under the impression that our postman told me one day that he had a letter addressed to Mr. Price, solicitor, at some number in Chester Street. I called subsequently at the address, and the housekeeper said letters so addressed were to be left there. I went to the post-office and mentioned the matter to one of the principal clerks, who said their instructions were to deliver all letters where they were addressed. Subsequently a smart-looking man called upon me and said the letter was for some relative of his who had been admitted in some American court, and that he himself was reader at the *Guardian* newspaper office, which latter fact I subsequently ascertained to be correct. I have inquired several times at the post-office if any more letters had been addressed to Mr. Price, solicitor, Chester Street, Shrewsbury, with a view of calling the attention of the Incorporated Law Society to the matter if I had found that such had been the case.

YOURS TRULY,

————

P.S. - I have always used plain paper without a printed address.

I NEED SCARCELY SAY that the writer of the letters and the "smart-looking gentleman" of the *Guardian* office were Mr. Foster, and that the address given was a cottage house, the rent of which was about 2s. 4d. per week, occupied by a railway porter, who was a widower, and with whose sister Foster had arranged that she should take in the letters, for which he gave her a small fee.

In November, 1886, I was off duty on my annual leave, and having returned from Buxton on account of the illness of my son and in Manchester, called at the Detective Office as I was passing, and in course of conversation with Mr. Superintendent Hicks learned that there had been a man in from the Colonies, giving the name of Tracey, and his address as 53, Carter Street, Greenheys, to report the loss of a bracelet worth £120, for the recovery of which he offered a reward of £20, but that he had called at the office again on the Saturday following and reported the discovery of the bracelet which he said had by some means become entangled in the dress of the lady who was wearing it.

Further conversation elicited the fact that the clerk who took the particulars noticed something suspicious about the man. I spoke to the clerk, who said the man was clean-shaven and wore a wig, looked like an actor, and resembled Henry Irving. Another suspicious circumstance was that, although he reported the loss of the bracelet, he was very anxious that no inquiries should be made respecting it at his house. On inquiring what Colony he was from, he said he came from San Francisco. I remarked, "That's rather a curious Colony." It appeared to me that Carter Street was not a neighbourhood where bracelets of the value of £120 were ordinarily found, and I remarked to the Superintendent, "If he lives in Carter Street, Greenheys, and says he has come from San Francisco, there is something 'dickey' about him, and inquiries should be made at once."

"Will you make them?" asked Mr. Hicks. "Yes, I will resume duty and go off to Carter Street immediately and endeavour to find out who he is."

On making inquiries in the neighbourhood I found the tenant of the house was a clerk, and that a person residing there in apartments was supposed to be connected with one of the pantomimes which were then preparing, and that he was a constant visitor to a house close by, where some theatrical ladies resided. Whilst watching the house I saw a man enter, and from the description given me at the office I took him to be the person who had given his name as Tracey.

At this time the American dynamitards were very busy,

and it struck me that if this person did come from San Francisco he might be in some way connected with them.

There are houses in Manchester which have been frequented by people of this kind for the past twelve or fourteen years and during the last five of that period men who are known to have been connected with the London explosions frequently visited Manchester, and were traced by me repeatedly from here to the Continent.

I at once set my usual sources of information at work, in the meantime keeping a close observation upon the premises. Having ascertained that there was nothing to fear in this direction I told the Superintendent on the following morning that I intended to borrow a bracelet from a firm of pawnbrokers and to go to Tracey with it. "What is the use of that?" he asked, "when he has got his bracelet back." "It will give me an introduction to the man," I replied, "and before I leave I will find out who he is."

Before I could carry out my arrangements I was sent for by a firm of solicitors who had another matter in hand, and on my return to the Town Hall to report where I was going I was called into the office of the superintendent, where I found Mr. Pingstone, a shopkeeper in Market Street, who, the superintendent informed me, had been giving some information respecting a man who had aroused his suspicions from the fact of his making very considerable purchases, for which he always paid in bank notes of large value; that he had been again that day and had made a small purchase, for which he tendered a £100 note, and that the man was to be back again in twenty minutes for the change, for which he, Mr. Pingstone, had sent to the bank.

The shopkeeper said that the man had given the name and address of George Tracey, of Carter Street, Greenheys, and looked like a priest, or an actor, and added, "But under no circumstances shall I take responsibility in the matter. Whatever you do, you will have to do it on your own account." As he continued the conversation, I recognised in the name and address that of the man I had been watching, and I was anxious to go on his track again and watch his movements in the City. When the shopkeeper ended a sentence with the news that he had sent the note to the bank to see if it was right - as he did not want any of us to come afterwards, and claim it from him if it turned out to be wrong - I said, "Very well, Mr. Pingstone, I will do my very best to serve you, but let us go or the man will be gone." As he did not wish to be seen with me, he walked on a few yards in front, but was evidently in a state of great excitement. He turned round several times on the way to his shop, which is only a short distance from the Town Hall, to tell me he would take no responsibility in the matter, and that "I must act on my own information." I impressed upon him the importance of getting on lest the man should disappear before we arrived at the shop; and I lagged behind a little so that he might not waste time in talking to me.

On arriving at the premises, the shopkeeper came out and informed me that the man had not yet arrived. About fifteen minutes later I observed "Tracey" go into the shop, for I at once recognised him as the man I had seen enter the house in Carter Street. When he came out I followed him, and, noticing that the shopkeeper was looking where I had gone, I waved my hand to his assistant, who was looking through the window, to indicate that I was on the track. I followed Tracey through several streets, saw him change and counter-change money at various shops, and with money-changers, and I stood beside him at the bullion office, at the Bank of England, while he changed money. He then hired a hansom, and drove first to the stage entrance of the Theatre Royal, and then to the Queen's Theatre, where he engaged a private box for the evening performance, afterwards driving to his lodgings in Greenheys.

I went back to the Town Hall and met the shopkeeper coming out with a gentleman. Turning away from the latter he asked, "Have you made anything of that, Caminada?"

"Yes!" I replied. "I am quite sure there is something wrong with the man. From what I have seen to-day, and what I have seen before, I intend to take him either to-day or in the course of a day or two."

Upon this he became very excited, flung his arms in the air, stamped his feet on the ground, and exclaimed, "You must not touch him on my information! If he turns out to be an honest man, the consequence will be most serious to me." "Do you think I am mad?" I asked, "to tell anyone the names of those who give me information? If I had to wait for definite information in every case, one half of the criminals would escape me."

It appears the shopkeeper was "a little bit indignant" at this conversation, "he being a member of the Corporation and I a servant of it;" or, as Mr. Justice Grantham afterwards put it, "he thought Jack was making himself as good as his master," and according to his own account "a little bit better too," upon which he "let me see that he was indignant and assumed an attitude of indignation."

Passing on, however, I noticed on turning my head that the shopkeeper appeared absorbed in thought; no doubt, as the judge suggested, he was thinking of actions for malicious prosecutions or something of that kind, so I stepped back and said, "As far as you are concerned in the matter you are dead." "That is what I want. I don't want my name brought into the matter in any way."

I then saw the Chief Constable and told him that I

suspected this man Tracey to be Foster, and I also repeated what Mr. Pingstone had just said. He told me to be cautious in what I did, and said I must not mention Mr. Pingstone's name in the affair. Mr. Superintendent Hicks also told me that Mr. Pingstone had just been in; that he was very excited; and that his name must not be mentioned to anyone.

I now assembled the whole of the clerks in the office, and procuring the *Police Gazette*, which contained a portrait of Foster, placed it before them and said, "Look at that portrait and tell me if it does not resemble the man who came to report the bracelet." They said it did not; and Mr. Superintendent Hicks also agreed that it was not the same man. One of the clerks remarked, "There is a clearer woodcut than that on a bill hanging in the parade room," and, on this being produced, they all persisted in saying it was not the same man.

It is only fair to explain that the description and the woodcut gave Foster a pair of bushy whiskers, while his face and head were now closely shaved, and he wore a wig. "Well," I said, "I believe he is the man." I put the bill, together with the portrait I cut from the *Police Gazette*, into my pocket, and started off again for Greenheys. I watched the house till six o'clock, when I was joined by Detective Wilson according to orders I had left, and about seven o'clock we saw "Tracey" leave the house in a brougham. We jumped into a cab at the corner of Oxford Street and followed; but before going very far the brougham was stopped, upon which our cab was pulled round. Getting out at the end of the street, I ran along the footpath, and on coming up close to the brougham saw Tracey enter the house where the theatrical ladies lived. He came out with one of them, who was engaged at a performance held in the

Free Trade Hall, and was known by the title of the "Vanishing Lady." They drove away together to the Queen's Theatre, to which place we followed them.

After they had got comfortably seated I left Wilson in charge of them, with instructions that he was not to lose sight of the man on any account, while I set off back again to his apartments in Carter Street. After some conversation with his landlady, I showed her the woodcut from the *Police Gazette*, and asked her if that resembled the man who resided in her house. "No, it does not; it is not the man, or at all like him." "How is he living?" I asked. "Very extravagantly," was the answer. "He may turn out to be a very disagreeable person. You tell me that he has come from America. It would be as well if I were to have a look into his boxes. I will take all the responsibility, and bear the brunt of any action that may be brought against you for allowing me to trespass in his apartments and search his boxes. In fact I will take every tittle of the responsibility, and give you an indemnity in writing, so that you need have no fear."

After satisfying her as to who I was, with a little persuasion she consented, and went with me to overhaul Mr. Tracey's boxes; but after examining everything of his that we could come across, except one box that was locked, I could find no trace of his identity, and I drove back to the Queen's Theatre.

I now submitted the portrait to Wilson, but he failed to recognise the man, and I said, "This is rather a serious undertaking. If this man is a straight 'un there will be 'ructions' in the Foreign Office, and there is no telling where we shall end if we once get among the red tape. What do you think about tackling him?" "Please yourself," he replied; "if you risk it I shall rely on your judgment."

The play was "The World," a Drury Lane drama, in

which the police have a long chase after a villain who has been concerned in the robbery of some valuable diamonds, and Tracey, who followed the plot of the piece and the fate of the diamonds with the closest interest, was apparently overjoyed at the triumph of the robber who effected his purpose by administering chloroform. As he leaned back in the box laughing, I looked again at the portrait and decided to arrest him.

After seeing the stage criminals disposed of, Tracey and his female companion lost no time in getting to their brougham. Calling Wilson to "come on," I got into the carriage after him, telling him that there was a little doubt in my mind as to his identity which could only be satisfactorily solved by a visit to the Town Hall. The lady upon this endeavoured to get out at one door and Tracey at the other; but getting Wilson into the cab I ordered the coachman to drive to the Town Hall. "Tracey" was very indignant and threatened all sorts of pains and penalties for the liberty I had taken, whilst the "vanishing lady" became hysterical. At the Detective Office I tried every means to induce him to admit who he really was. I asked him if he could refer me to any respectable person in Manchester, or elsewhere, or whether he had a banking account; but the only information I could get from him was that he was known to the jeweller from whom he purchased the bracelet, and which I found upon the arm of the "vanishing lady." He admitted, however, that the jeweller knew nothing of him further than the purchase of the bracelet. Upon this I charged him with being "Foster." I asked for a telegraph form and wrote upon it before him:-

"To the Chief Constable, Birmingham. Send Bradley, solicitor, here at once. Suspect Foster in custody. Chief Constable, Manchester."

I then said to the prisoner, "We are going to keep you until Mr. Bradley comes. See the condition of the lady; she is going to faint. If you are not the man say who you are."

As I was handing over the telegram for the purpose of being forwarded, he said, "I am the man!" On this the lady was released, and after Foster was locked up I proceeded again to his apartments in Greenheys, where I found in the box which was locked £3,826 in gold.

About 11.30 the next morning the shopkeeper and Councillor Mainwaring came to me in the City Police Court with a request that I would get him (Pingstone) a good place where he could see Foster without being seen himself. I said there was no such place, but I would find him a comfortable seat, when the court officer who brought him to me intimated that he would place him behind the door of the Magistrate's entrance to the bench, which contains two glass panes with silk curtains drawn across. Behind these he stood, with one of the curtains drawn across, like "Peeping Tom of Coventry," watching the proceedings during the examination; but it was amusing to see how quickly he vanished when Foster made any movement with his eyes in that direction.

The same morning I spoke to the Chief Constable, and hoped he would speak to Mr. Pingstone about the assistance he had given us; and I recommended that when the case came to be settled a handsome gratuity should be given to his shopman.

The following report appeared in the *Standard* of the proceedings when Foster was brought up at Bow Street Police Station:-

"ARTHUR FOSTER, 33, clerk, was charged with obtaining £5,200, by means of forgery and fraud.

Mr. J. T. White said his firm was the London agent of Mr. Isaac Bradley, solicitor, Colmore Row, Birmingham. On November 1st he received a letter from Mr. Bradley, authorising his firm to pay sums received by them on account of certain estates to Mr. Walter Nicholls, son of one of the parties, amounting in the whole to £5,200. The letter referred in detail to the several estates on account of which payment was to be made, and enclosed a specimen of the signature of Walter Nicholls. Witness's firm was to draw an open cheque, and to take the signature of Walter Nicholls, who, further to prove his identity, was to present an address card bearing Mr. Bradley's name. On the day this letter was received the prisoner called, presented Mr. Bradley's card, and said he was Walter Nicholls. Witness drew a cheque on the London and Westminster Bank for £5,200, which had been returned paid.

Mr. Isaac Bradley, solicitor, Birmingham, said Messrs. White and Sons were his London agents. The prisoner entered his employ in June as shorthand clerk, and left without giving or receiving notice on October 30th. The letter marked B (produced), signed Isaac Bradley and addressed to Messrs. White and Sons, was not his writing. The body of the letter was in the writing of the prisoner, and so was the authority to receive the £5,200, which was apparently signed by Samuel Nicholls and William Cromley, as well as witnessed by himself; all the three signatures were forgeries. Another authority to receive the money produced and marked E was in the writing of the prisoner, and the signature, Isaac Bradley, was a forgery.

Jerome Caminada, Chief Inspector of the Manchester

detectives, said about eleven at night, on the 6th inst., he apprehended the prisoner as he was leaving the Queen's Theatre, Bridge Street, Manchester. Prisoner entered a brougham with a lady, and witness followed him in, and told him he had reason to believe he was wanted at Birmingham for extensive forgeries, and that as it was a serious matter he should order the driver to go to the Town Hall for inquiries. They were driven there accordingly, when witness told the prisoner he had seen him about noon enter the Bank of England and there change notes into gold. He had also seen him afterwards change notes for gold at the shops of money changers, in Deansgate, Cross Street, and near the Exchange, and had seen him enter a house, No. 53, Carter Street, Greenheys, and another house in the same street, where a lady resided. Witness produced a photograph of the man wanted, and said to him, "Do you deny being the man?" He replied, "No, I do not; but let the lady go. She knows nothing about it." Upon searching the prisoner witness found £320 in notes, £12 10s. in gold, 14 s. 6d. in silver, a gold watch, and two diamond rings. He also received from the lady, in the prisoner's presence, two diamond bracelets, a diamond ring, gold and pearl earrings, gold necklet, and gold watch, which, with one exception, she said the prisoner had given to her. On searching the prisoner's apartments he found in a leather portmanteau £3,800 in gold, and in a small leather bag £26. He also took possession of all the prisoner's clothes. Prisoner made no reply when the charge was read to him, and witness brought him to London.

The prisoner was remanded to Tuesday.

Mr. Vaughan said Inspector Caminada was entitled to exceeding credit for the manner in which he had effected the arrest of the prisoner."

Ultimately Foster was sentenced to 14 years' penal servitude. The sum of £333 4s. 6d. had been found upon him when arrested, and £3,826 was recovered at his lodgings. The total amount was £4,159 4s. 6d. Of this £4,159 was paid into the Bank of England, King Street, on the 23rd of December, 1886, to the credit of Mr. Bradley, the balance, 3s. 8d., being charged at the bank for light gold.

21

"SMASHERS," OR BASE COIN
"PITCHERS" OR TENDERERS

One evening after leaving the Detective Office, about half-past nine, I walked along Deansgate with a brother officer. It was during Easter week; and those who have any remembrance of old Knott Mill Fair will know the kind of pandemonium into which the neighbourhood was turned during that festival. Deansgate was lined with nut and gingerbread stalls, "try your weight" and "strength" machines, "throwing the ring" for walking sticks or knives, lotteries for various articles, stalls with "all on the board one penny," ballad singers, with travelling auctioneers here and there, plying their calling, making the scene a busy one, and filling the air with a perfect Babel of sounds.

After bidding my brother officer good-night, I proceeded along Deansgate, and had not gone far before I noticed two young men standing by the side window of a druggist's shop, in such a way as to screen themselves from the light. It seemed to me that there was something suspicious about their manner; so, taking up a position between the house and the shop door of a grocer's shop, in the shadow of the buildings, whilst the street was ablaze with gas and naphtha lamps, I set myself to watch them.

I had not to wait long before I saw something pass from one to the other. The man who had received the article then went across the street and made a purchase at a gingerbread stall. Some altercation took place between the buyer and the seller, which was evidently watched with great interest by the companion of the former from the opposite side of the street, and after he had left the stall he joined him. Just at this time an officer in uniform was coming in the direction in which they were going, and I seized them both, calling upon the officer to assist me.

We were not above one hundred and fifty yards from the Knott Mill Police Station. As I noticed the one I had hold of fumbling with his brace as we went along - he said it had come unfastened - I called to the officer to watch the other prisoner and see that he did not drop anything.

At the Police Station we searched the prisoners, and in the vest pocket of the one who was held by the officer we found a base coin, which he admitted he had offered in payment for the purchase he made at the stall, but explained that he had picked it up in the street and did not know it was a bad one.

Knowing that these passers of base coin worked in couples - one holding the "swag," or bag containing the stock, whilst the "smasher," or "pitcher," took one at a time, so that in case of detection no more than one could be found upon him, and thus make his conviction difficult, unless other cases could be proved against him - and seeing from the manner of the prisoners that there was something which I had not found out, I again searched them both thoroughly; but in vain.

Determined, however, not to be beaten, I began to strip

them, when I found attached to the brace of one of them a string which had been fastened in such a way that it could be slipped loose on the slightest pull. By some means or other the string had become twisted and knotted, and therefore did not act. Tracing this string down the leg of the prisoner's trousers, I found at the end a bag containing a very large number of base coins, all wrapped carefully in tissue paper and ready for tendering. Of course the object was plain. Had the string not become knotted, but had worked properly, the bag would have fallen down the prisoner's trousers into the street, probably unperceived. Thus he might have escaped the serious charge of having in his possession a quantity of base coin, and conviction would have been made more difficult against the other.

Both prisoners were sent for trial at the Assizes, where they were found guilty, on the 27th of July, 1874, and each sentenced to five years' penal servitude and three years' police supervision, having been previously convicted of a similar offence.

22

GAMBLING HELLS

BETTING-HOUSE RAIDS

I n the year 1869 the betting nuisance had reached a great height in Manchester, and it was carried on openly in most of the public-houses and small beer-houses of the city. The neighbourhood of Thomas Street was its headquarters, and in a yard near, called "Tattersall's," a great concourse of people assembled every day, comprised chiefly of clerks, warehousemen, porters, mechanics, and other working-men.

The authorities having come to the conclusion to put down this state of things, I was ordered to make inquiries, and these led to an extensive raid being carried out on Whit-Monday, 1869. After the procession of scholars had passed, the police were collected, as was usual, under Chief Super-intendent Gee, but instead of being marched to their respec-tive stations they were taken to St. Paul's Churchyard, which was then in Turner Street, in the neighbourhood of the betting centres. From here raids were simultaneously made upon the betting houses situated in the neighbourhood of Thomas Street, and I succeeded in getting convictions in about nineteen cases, fines being imposed varying from £75 to £100, and amounting in the aggregate to £1,350.

Between this and the year 1881 I had several similar cases. In the latter year the Chief Constable instructed me to institute an inquiry into the proceedings of these betting clubs, and to have my report in readiness in case any action should be decided upon. In 1882, and August, 1883, the subject was considered. In 1884 I again submitted my report of those proceedings, which was very strongly worded as to the growing evils of the betting nuisance. Complaints being constantly received, further inquiries were instituted, and in February, 1885, the Chief Constable again asked for my report.

This was duly submitted and considered. It was then decided to take action at the commencement of the Lincoln Race Meeting in the following month, and everything was got in readiness for the purpose; but certain utterances were incautiously made about this time by a prominent public man, an ex-mayor of the city, in which he described the gambling dens, and said that something must be done to suppress them. This caused quite a flutter among the betting fraternity and frustrated our plans.

Time had now to be given for the excitement to tame down before the scheme could be carried out, and the interval was used in obtaining evidence that would place beyond doubt the illegal nature of the practices indulged in by the members of the betting clubs. With this object steps were taken to maintain a careful watch upon a large number of the resorts of the sporting fraternity.

With one club, for which a very odd situation had been chosen, I had some difficulty. This was the Burton Club, held in a large room over a saw mill, which stood back from City Road in the middle of a yard. I made many efforts to ascertain what was taking place in this club, but without success, until I thought of a particular applicant who wished to enter the police force. He had obtained work at the "Skittle Alley," a place well known in Manchester as the resort of loose characters, which opened about eleven o'clock in the evening and closed about one o'clock in the morning. The owner of this club was a boot and shoe maker, and the assistant at the "Skittle Alley," following my instructions, took to him an old shoe to repair. After getting into conversation with him my representative drew from his pocket a copy of the *Sporting Chronicle*, and asked the boot-maker if he had anything good for that day's races. In the course of conversation the engagement at the "Skittle Alley" was mentioned, and Mr. Burton was invited to call some night as some business might be done amongst the young swells. This was enough. The heart of Mr. Burton immediately warmed towards this new friend; his mind was at once filled with visions of the wealth that was to accrue to him from the pockets of the young spendthrifts, through his friend of the "Skittle Alley," and on the strength of it he rushed him off to the club, made him a member, and stood him drinks.

The "Skittle Alley" man also successfully used similar tactics in another case, taking lodgings near the premises.

When information had been obtained which it was believed would secure the conviction of those most closely concerned in the management of these clubs, the time and mode of action were arranged. This was done with the greatest possible secrecy.

No member of the police force, or of the detective department, beyond the Chief Constable, the Deputy Chief Constable, Superintendent Hicks, and myself, was aware until they received their orders after they had been paraded at noon on the day of the raid as to what was the class of duty in which they were about to be engaged.

The 20th of May, 1885, was decided on as presenting an exceptionally favourable opportunity for making the raid, inasmuch as it was the second day of the Newmarket Spring Meeting, upon one event of which - the race for the Payne Stakes - great interest was centred, and two o'clock was fixed upon as the hour when the bookmakers would be in the height of their business.

Between a quarter and half-past one on this day, certain men with whom I had been working in the clubs were ordered to give me information by signal as to how things were proceeding. This they did without knowing what my intentions were, and on finding from their reports that everything was in full swing, I immediately made up my mind and proceeded to put the force in motion. It was seen that a large body of men would be needed to surround twenty-two clubs, each full of an assemblage of men who might be expected to resist an intrusion unless the police were present in sufficient force.

Accordingly orders were issued for a preliminary inspection parade, and over 400 men were collected at their respective divisional stations for this ostensible purpose. Shortly after one o'clock these orders were countermanded, messengers were sent to headquarters with instructions to each division, and with warrants authorising various Inspectors to enter those clubs which had been elected for visitation, to detain all persons engaged in betting and gambling, and to search for and seize all instruments of unlawful gaming under the directions so conveyed.

The force was divided into sections, each deemed powerful enough to make certain the execution of the warrant at the individual club for which it was now intended, and the departure of the sections was so planned that the invasion of the clubs should be accomplished simultaneously.

Most of these clubs communicated with each other by means of telephones, and such was the precision with which the raid was carried out that on a telephone message being sent from one club to another to apprise its members of what was taking place in their neighbourhood the other found itself in the same predicament. In fact, such was the success of the raid that every one of the twenty-two clubs was surrounded and every person upon the premises detained. Simultaneously with the departure of the police from the various stations, I, with five other officers, set out for the purpose of arresting the officials of the clubs and the bookmakers under the warrants with which the officers who accompanied the main force were provided.

The first clubs attacked were the "Rous" and the "Falmouth," the first on the ground floor and the second on the third floor of a building in Macdonald's Lane, which was reached by a winding staircase. We found upon the premises over 200 men, and a fearful scene ensued as we entered. Seeing me coming they closed the door, and, as they refused to open it, I broke it open. There was a general scramble on the part of the betting men to get their betting books, money, and other articles out of sight, and on the part of the members to get out of the place. While the police were endeavouring to push their way up the stairs to the "Falmouth," the betting men were rushing down, some of them jumping from top to bottom over the heads of those below, and making considerable trade for hatters. Several made their escape out of the window, and one unfortunate man jumped on the sky-light above the "Rous," and the roof giving way he fell into the club, and then jumped through a window out of the building. In doing so he received a terrible cut in the calf of the leg and had to be taken to the infirmary by two police officers. Others ran along the sky-light over the commercial room of the Falstaff Hotel, breaking the glass and cutting themselves more or less severely, and for a quarter of an hour the scene was one of indescribable confusion, and the falling of glass causing considerable consternation below.

As soon as I could get a hearing I ascended the bar and proceeded to read out the warrant. I announced that it was not the intention of the Chief Constable to take into custody all those found upon the premises, but only those who were responsible for the betting business carried on. These were the officials and servants of the place, together with the bookmakers and their clerks, and if they would give them-selves up no disturbance need be made.

On hearing this intimation many of those present became more reconciled, and some degree of order was obtained. After a little while, the men having had time to cool down, the request was readily complied with. Having secured the principals at one end of the room, the rest were allowed to disperse, and thankful they were to think they had been allowed to escape.

The principals were taken into custody, and about a score in number were escorted to the Town Hall through an immense crowd which had by this time congregated, a policeman paying particular attention to each of the prisoners.

By this time the whole of the city was roused and became alive to what was going on, and as I and my colleagues went from club to club, arresting the leading men and sending them to join their companions at the

Town Hall, we were followed by a large crowd shouting, cheering, yelling, and making as much noise as possible.

At some of the clubs immense crowds had congregated by the time we arrived, and we had some difficulty in pushing our way through the roughs who shouted, cheered, and hissed at us. The liberated members of the clubs fared little better, for they were received with shouts, chaffs, and remarks more or less complimentary and consoling, as they came out.

At the Palmerston Club, Ardwick, a notorious character jumped through the window and made his escape at the back, while the police were entering the front, and at the Pin Mill Club - a dirty little place close to, with scarcely room for a dozen men to turn round - the husband of a woman who had charge of the bar left her with the remark, "Never mind, lass, it will be all right, as Bill Hayes will pay," as her only consolation.

Another of the clubs, the Devonshire, was situated over a stable, and approached by a wooden step-ladder from a coach-house and store-house. This secret den had been a favourite betting place for the wives of working men in the neighbourhood. The director, bookkeeper, secretary and treasurer, all combined in one, was a big Falstaff-proportioned man, who had evidently fattened on his gains. This club boasted no less than 370 members, who had paid an annual subscription of one shilling each.

In Deansgate, crowds of the dirty low-looking inhabitants of this haunt of vice had congregated. The Central Club, in Back Lad Lane, a resort for the rough characters of the neighbourhood, consisted of a large room, open to the roof, with a dirty saw-dust floor, containing a rickety billiard table. About seventy men were found there, half a dozen of whom were taken into custody, including three very "horsey-looking" juvenile bookmakers, one of whom - "Young Cheeky" - insisted upon helping himself to a thick cigar, a drink, and a meat pie, tucking the pie under his coat before accepting the arm of his escort policeman.

Many of the "gentry" of these clubs, however, were far too respectable to walk, and in cabs hired at their own expense they drove with the police to the Town Hall. At the Lancashire Club, off Hyde Road, an immense and most disorderly crowd had assembled outside the premises, and they had persuaded two or three itinerant musicians to blurt out the strain of "Auld Lang Syne" as our cabs drove up.

The "band" played a jaunty tune while the proceedings inside the club were going on, and when the three officials who were taken into custody were being brought away the musicians put additional enthusiasm into "We'll run 'em in."

The general result of this raid showed that in many cases these clubs had been carried on by one man, who had assumed to himself all the offices required to carry it on. In small dingy rooms clubs had been carried on with from 300 to 400 members, paying from one shilling to three shillings per year subscription.

They were all fitted up with telephones or telegraph instruments, billiard, or semi-billiard tables, bars, and all the usual accessories. The characters arrested were as a rule noticeable more for their youth and thoroughly depraved condition than for their respectability. A number of well-dressed people were found upon the premises in the centre of the city, and these were only too anxious to get away and hide their shame. It was deplorable to find that quite a large number of women and young lads had acquired the habit of visiting the clubs, some of which had become notorious for this evil. The number of persons found upon the premises of the clubs at the time of the raid was over 2,000, but only about 200 were taken to the Town Hall.

In the evening, all but forty-five of them were set at liberty, and before midnight these were liberated on bail, or on entering into their own recognisances to come up for trial. Some idea of the amount of betting that was in progress when the police entered the clubs may be gathered from the fact that, in addition to the money found upon the premises, £2,200 was found in the pockets of those who were apprehended.

At many of the clubs gambling by means of cards was extensively carried on, and in one case the members were known to make a practice of commencing to play on a Saturday afternoon, and continuing it until Sunday morning.

These clubs were purely bogus ones. Though the form of registering had been gone through, no company in the true sense of the word existed. The "Limited Company" was comprised of one man, and a few friends had lent their names for the purpose of registration. They were in many cases got up for the proprietors by a person named F__, a hatter, who afterwards kept a newspaper shop, when he was fined for betting. He then became secretary to a betting club, and derived some very handsome fees for his services. In some cases the proprietors of these clubs were well-to-do men, carrying on extensive business in the city, and having suburban residences. One of these gentlemen was an iron merchant in one of the principal thoroughfares. Besides the profit from his business, he had an income of £7 per week from his wife, with a suburban residence at Sale, in Cheshire, and yet he was proprietor of the miserable premises already described as the Pin Mill Club. He was fined £35 for carrying on betting there.

Most of the clubs had an admirable set of rules. For instance, the objects of one were to "afford tradesmen and others the means of social intercourse and mutual helpfulness by providing a place of business and recreation, combined with the comforts of a home."

These "comforts" were promoted by means of an old cottage up an entry in Fennell Street. There was a very dark and ill-paved yard to go through, and then you went up some steps into a cottage, the only part of which was used were two rooms on the ground floor. In one of these there was a barrel of beer and a table, and in the other, in one corner, a little bar, behind which there were usually about two gallons of spirits, and in another corner there was a small table. With the exception of a form or two and a few chairs, these were all the means the club had for "social intercourse and helpfulness" and the "comforts of a home." In no single case was their provision for the election of members carried out. Practically, all anyone had to do was to go up and say he wanted to be a member, and by paying a small sum he became one.

In all these cases proceedings had been taken under the Act passed in the 16th and 17th year of Her Majesty Queen Victoria, c. 119, entitled - "An Act for the Suppression of Betting Houses." In the case of the club in the entry off Fennell Street, such items appeared in the cash book as "won on the week, £16 4s. 6d.; won on the week, £49 5s. 4d."

Convictions followed in each case, and fines were inflicted ranging from £25 to £100, with extra costs, making a total in fines of about £3,000.

THE SPORTING CHRONICLE, in a description of the proceedings at the Manchester City Police Court, on the 22nd June, 1885, said:-

"THE EVIDENCE PRODUCED WAS the same in each case. William Gregory, 'a police constable,' was a singularly weak specimen of that somewhat robust order. He wore spectacles, was sparely built, did not look more than 20 years of age, and he would have been a clever, circumspect janitor indeed who could have seen the prying 'police constable' in William, or 'N.E.' as he gave his name at the various places where he had been enrolled as a member. Arthur Evans, a solicitor's clerk, as he described himself, was even a younger-looking 'artist' than his brother witness. He had more of the appearance of a big shock-headed lad, a very 'fresh caught one,' than an aspiring Vidocq, or one covetous of following in the footsteps of clever Jerome Caminada. The third witness was Elijah Davies, a betting tipster, a man of much maturer years than the other two instruments of the police, and whose face was not one which anyone would suspect was one of the detective staff.

"At the Lancashire Club one of the men who found himself in the position of the defendants had his suspicions previously aroused that all was not as it should be with Davies, but on asking Evans, as he styles himself when in the pursuit of a calling for which he seems to have great natural attainments, that youth allayed his nervous doubts with a string of what he confessed, in cross-examination, were several lies. On the evidence given by these three men - Gregory, Evans, and Davies - the police arrested all the cases gone into. To those who were versed in racing matters, the idea must have struck home that the racing knowledge of the witnesses was not of 'yesterday.' In going their rounds for the purposes of prosecution, all three men backed winners, including Redskin, who started at 8 to 1 for the Esher Stakes, Jolly Sir John, Preferment, and Chopette colt at 6 to 1 for a place in the Two Thousand Guineas. If these bets were the selection of 'novices' - people who, so to speak, were playing at a game they did not understand - then all that can be said is that they were exceedingly lucky in picking winners. This fact impressed the crowd, which smiled audibly as the bets transpired in evidence. Caminada also appeared in the witness-box against each set of defendants, but what he had to say was in relation to the premises, and the 'articles of accusation' found on them, rather than the business carried on by the accused. The celebrated Manchester detective, whose name and fame are known from one end of England to the other, is nothing very dreadful to look at; indeed, some people might describe him - and with truth - as a pleasant little man. He might be a trifle over 5ft. 7in. in height, but not much more, while his weight, at a rough guess, would be 12st. or 13st. Caminada wears a moustache, and a thin fringing beard and whiskers give the impression that a razor has seldom, if ever, visited his broad, good-humoured face, while he parts his hair down the centre, and does not appear to have a particle of ill-nature about him.

"Under examination Caminada's answers come out short, sharp, and decisive, with a certain 'snap' about his words as if he was putting handcuffs on everything he says, to make his replies thoroughly secure. He has in every instance a clear tale to tell, with powers of terse description, and a condensed summing up of what he sees and does which are simply perfect. No hesitation was shown in any of his answers, and a hearty laugh went up at a quick offer which he made to give up some notes to Mr. Cottingham.

There was no unfair pressing of the case against the defendants, and anything that could tell in their favour was said. He frankly said of one of the 'unfortunates' that 'he had known him for a good many years, and had known him as a very respectable man.' There was, however, not the ghost of a chance for the chief men summoned in the first two cases, and, electing to be tried there and then, they were very heavily fined."

In April, 1888, complaints were received of annoyance caused by the proceedings which were continually taking place at a certain club in the neighbourhood of Cheetham, and after making inquiries and obtaining sufficient evidence upon which to act, I applied for a warrant, which was granted. About half-an-hour after midnight I proceeded one Sunday morning, accompanied by about thirty detectives, to the premises, and arrested a considerable number of men and women, who were all taken to the Town Hall, where the majority of the prisoners were admitted to bail on their own recognisances, that of the principals being fixed at two sureties of £50 each, and their own recognisances of £50. The charge was laid under the 17th and 18th Victoria, chap. 38, sec.4, which provides that persons keeping a common gaming house, or assisting in the management of such a house shall be liable to a fine not exceeding £500, or be imprisoned for not longer than twelve months.

It was proved that the club was used solely for gambling purposes, so much an hour being charged for cards, and that in baccarat the banker paid 1s. for each deal; that a card committee was appointed to settle all disputes; and that it was usual for play to commence on Saturday night and continue until Monday morning without intermission. All this was proved by detectives who relieved one another during the interval.

There were constant disputes, and these led to brawling, bad language, and fighting. There was also a considerable number of cases in which charges of cheating were made, and in some cases these were substantiated.

The prisoners elected to be tried by a jury, and at the June Sessions, 1888, fines were imposed on the principal prisoners varying from £10 to £50, with £5 costs in each case.

The following is a copy of the Warrant in connection with these raids:-

"To JEROME CAMINADA, of the City of Manchester, Chief Inspector of Detective Police.

"Whereas it appears to me, Francis John Headlam, Stipendiary Magistrate, acting in and for the said city, by the information upon oath of Jerome Caminada, of the city, Chief Inspector of Detective Police, that a place known by the name of ___, and situate in Mount Street, in the said city, is kept and used as a betting house within the meaning of an Act passed in the sixteenth and seventeenth years of the reign of Her present Majesty, Chapter one hundred and nineteen, entitled an Act for the Suppression of Betting Houses.

"This is, therefore, in the name of our Lady the Queen to require you with such assistance as you may find necessary, to enter into the said place, and, if necessary, to use force for the purpose of making such entry, whether by breaking open doors, or otherwise, and there diligently to search for all instruments of unlawful gaming, and to seize all lists, cards, or other documents relating to racing or betting found in such place or premises, and to arrest, search, and bring before me, or some other Justice of the Peace of our Lady the Queen assigned to keep the peace within the said city, as well as the keepers of the same, as also the persons there haunting, resorting, playing, and betting, to be dealt with according to law, and for so doing this shall be your Warrant.

"Given under my hand and seal at the said city this 4th day of ___, in the year of our Lord one thousand eight hundred and eighty-five.

"FRANCIS J. HEADLAM."

GLOSSARY

Base: fake
Beak: magistrate, judge
Bloke-buzzer: pickpocket
Cracksman: safebreaker
'D': detective
Dibs: money
Fence: receiver of stolen property
Flat: easily deceived person
Gamp: umbrella
Greenhorn: a gullible person who is easily tricked
Pitcher: passer of false money
Ringing the changes: con trick involving exchanging coins for change
Sharper, sharp: swindler who uses cards
Smasher: passer of false money
Snaps: handcuffs
Swell: well-dressed gentleman
Welsher: one who receives money to place a bet on a horse and then absconds without paying

BOOKS BY ANGELA BUCKLEY

The Real Sherlock Holmes: The Hidden Story of Jerome Caminada

The Victorian Super-sleuth Investigates series:

Amelia Dyer and the Baby Farm Murders

Who Killed Constable Cock?

THE REAL SHERLOCK HOLMES

THE HIDDEN STORY OF JEROME CAMINADA

By Angela Buckley

As seen in The Telegraph, The Times and on The One Show

A master of disguise with a keen eye for detail and ingenious methods of deduction, Detective Caminada pursued notorious criminals through the seedy streets of Victorian Manchester's underworld. Known as a 'terror to evil-doers', he stalked pickpockets and thieves, ruthless con artists and cold-blooded killers.

Bearing all the hallmarks of Sir Arthur Conan Doyle, this compelling story establishes Detective Caminada as a true Victorian super-sleuth and a real-life Sherlock Holmes. Published by Pen & Sword.

'A gripping new book' - Manchester Evening News

'A treat for inquisitive readers' - The Crime Readers' Association

'A highly enjoyable book' - The Whitechapel Society

Printed in Poland
by Amazon Fulfillment
Poland Sp. z o.o., Wrocław